T
ITS HISTORY, MANUFACTURE

AND USE

BY

HENRY SAINT-GEORGE

PREFACE.

It has always appeared to me a curious thing that the bow, without which the fiddle could have no being, should have received so scant attention, not alone from the community of fiddlers, but also from writers on the subject. I only know of one book in which the subject is adequately handled. Out of every twenty violinists who profess to some knowledge of the various types of Cremonese and other fiddles of repute and value, barely three will be met with who take a similar interest in the bow beyond knowing a good one, or rather one that suits their particular physique, when playing with it. They are all familiar with the names of Dodd and Tourte, but it is seldom that their knowledge extends beyond the names. As for a perception of the characteristics of bows as works of art, which is the standard of the fiddle connoisseur, it hardly has any existence outside the small circle of bow makers. Of the large number of undoubted fiddle experts now in London, but a small proportion profess to any similar knowledge of bows, and of these there are but few who can be credited with real authority in the matter.

It is, therefore, with the object of bringing the bow into more general notice that this little book has been written, and, to drop into the good old prefatory style, if I succeed in arousing the interest of but one violinist in the bow for itself, and apart from its work, my efforts will not have been in vain.

My most hearty thanks are due to those who have so kindly assisted me in my work. To *Messrs. W. E. Hill and Sons, Mr. E. Withers, Mr. F. W. Chanot, Mr. J. Chanot, and Messrs. Beare, Goodwin and Co.*, for the loan of valuable bows for the purpose of illustration, and *Mr. A. Tubbs*, who, in addition to similar favours, most kindly placed much of his valuable time at my disposal, and very patiently helped me to a sufficient understanding of the bow maker's craft for the purpose of collecting materials for the second part of the book.

The third part, in which I treat of the use of the bow, I have purposely avoided making a systematic handbook of bowing technique, for to handle that subject as exhaustively as I should wish would require a separate volume. As stated in Chapter XIV., that portion of the book is addressed almost exclusively to teachers, and in the few cases where I have gone into questions of technique it has been limited to those points that appear to be most neglected or misunderstood by the generality of teachers.

"Anything that is worth doing is worth doing well" is a maxim that teachers should hold up to themselves and their pupils, and this reminds me of an exhortation to that effect in "Musick's Monument," that quaint and pathetic book of Thomas Mace (1676) with which I cannot do better than end my already too extensive preamble.

"Now being Thus far *ready* for *Exercise*, attempt the *Striking of your Strings;* but before you do *That*, Arm yourself with Preparative *Resolutions to gain a Handsome—Smooth—Sweet—Smart—Clear—Stroak;* or else Play not at all."

PART I.
THE HISTORY OF THE BOW.

CHAPTER I.

ORIGIN OF INSTRUMENTS—FRICTIONAL VIBRATION—THE BOW DISTINCT FROM THE PLECTRUM—THE TRIGONON—BOWING WITH VARIOUS OBJECTS.

As has been observed by the most talented writer on this subject "the history of the bow is practically that of the violin." It will therefore be readily understood that in the earlier portions of this *opusculum* it will be impossible to separate them to any great extent; also, I must crave my readers' indulgence for going over a considerable tract of already well trodden ground. My excuse must be my desire for completeness, for, as I propose to deal with the evolution of the modern bow, I find it difficult to arbitrarily select a starting point to the exclusion of all previous details, whether of ascertained fact or conjecture. Therefore I will follow the invariable custom of fiddle literature and go back to the regions of speculative history for a commencement.

Speculative history is, I fear, more fascinating to the writer than convincing to the reader, so I will be as brief as possible in this particular, nor will I, like one John Gunn who wrote a treatise on fingering the violoncello, fill up space with irrelevant matter such as the modes and tunings of the ancient Greek lyres, etc., highly interesting as these subjects may be, although it is a very tempting method of getting over the "bald and unconvincing" nature of the bow's early history.

We of the present generation, having the bow in its most perfect form, are apt to take its existence for granted; we do not think that there must have been a period when no such thing was known, and, consequently, fail to appreciate the difficulties in the way of its discovery or invention. With some other instruments it is different. For wind instruments we have a prototype in the human voice, and one may reasonably suppose that the trumpet class were evolved by slow process from the simple action of placing the hands on either side of the mouth to augment a shout. The harp may have been suggested by the twanging of a bow-string as an arrow left the archer's hand, and a seventeenth century play writer fancifully attributed the invention of string instruments to the finding of a "dead horse head." Here, of course, would be found a complete resonance-chamber and possibly some dried and stretched sinews—quite sufficient to suggest lute-like instruments to men of genius such as must have formed a much larger proportion of the world's population in prehistoric times than is the case to-day; for brilliant as our great men of art and science are, there are few who can be called *originators* in the simplest meaning of the word.

Thus, then, we have wind instruments, harps and lutes; but the bow eludes us. If we are determined to find a suggestion in nature we must turn to certain insects of the cricket and grasshopper tribe. Many of these, in particular the locusts, are thorough fiddlers, using their long hind-leg as a bow across the edge of the hollow wing-case to produce the familiar chirping sound.

FIG. 1.

Naturally, the strings are absent, but here is to be found a perfect example of the excitation of frictional vibration. Whether this was actually what suggested the bow is another matter.

For my own part, while admitting that in close observation of nature our early forefathers were probably supreme, I prefer to think that the innate concept of the bow was latent in the human mind and only waited some fortunate accident of observation to start it into being.

I am aware, however, that this is a highly unscientific position to take up.

That there should be so little in the way of adequate record concerning the development of this indispensable adjunct of the violin is not a matter for great wonderment, for, as has elsewhere been shown, the earlier bowed instruments were of such primitive construction, and, consequently, so weak in tone that they were totally unsuited to the purposes of ceremonial or pageantry; two subjects which form prominent features in ancient pictorial representations. And if we come to what we fondly term "more civilized" times, we find such crude drawings of early viols and kindred instruments that we must not be surprised if such an apparently unimportant detail as the bow should receive still more perfunctory treatment at the hands of the artist.

We must also remember that the word "fiddlesticks" is still applied to anything that is beneath contempt in its utter lack of importance.

Undoubtedly the idea of exciting vibrations in a stretched string by means of friction is one of great antiquity; so much so, indeed, that the question of origin becomes merely one of conjecture. True, the majority of writers look upon the bow as a development of the *plectrum*, but this is a theory that I must confess does not strike me as being satisfactorily probable. To paraphrase a popular expression, "fingers were made before *plectra*," the latter being an "improvement" on nature's contrivance. And I see no reasonable objection to the supposition that friction may have been used as a means of tone-production prior to the introduction of the *plectrum*.

The great dissimilarity between the producing of sound by plucking, and that by friction is such that I see no occasion to evolve one from the other and consider their introduction most probably coeval.

When we come to the direct percussion of a string, as in the dulcimer, piano, etc., we at once perceive a possible connection between the hammer of the one and the rod or bow of the other: the accidental colliding of the bow with the strings of its accompanying instrument would soon suggest experiments ending in the forming of dulcimer-like instruments.* But if we grant that the art of plucking a string had first advanced as far as the substitution of a *plectrum* for what Mace calls the "nibble end of the flesh," I fail to see how such an implement could suggest the friction of a string, as, if short enough for manipulation in its original use, it would not be long enough to excite the continuous vibrations characteristic of the bow.

* The bow is frequently used now as a means of percussion for certain effects.

I do not accept the theory of a long *plectrum* used for pizzicato purposes, as I consider, with Engel, that such an implement would have been unmanageably clumsy even for the primitive music of the ancients. Whenever I see a rod, as in the accompanying drawing of the Assyrian Trigonon, I maintain that its purpose was to excite frictional vibrations.

FIG. 2.

FIG. 3.

The method of performance readily suggests itself in this case as it will be seen that it would be quite possible and convenient for the player to pass his rod—probably a rough surfaced reed—*between* the strings. I do not think it could have been used for percussion as, in that case, it would surely have had some hammer like projection at its end; a salient feature hardly to be missed by the artist as were the less obtrusive details of the true bow in later ages.

We are all familiar with the oft repeated anecdote of Paganini's playing with a light reed-stem, and I remember having seen at Christmas festivities in country homesteads, the village fiddler playing a brisk old-time tune with the long stem of his clay pipe; also, quite recently, I read an account of an "artiste" in the States who charmed his enlightened audiences with his performances on the violin by using a variety of heterogeneous objects in lieu of the conventional bow, including a stick of sealing-wax and a candle!

Now I do not wish to prove that the implement held by the benign Assyrian in Fig. 2, is either of the last named articles, but merely to draw attention to the fact that friction-tone is producible without the aid of a "bow" proper.

The use of plain reed stems or other suitable rods for the production of continuous sounds would naturally soon give place to more elaborately constructed implements; although Rühlmann gives a drawing of a portion of the sculptured decorations that adorn the famous "Golden Porch" at Freiburg which represents a crwth and bow of the twelfth century, the bow being merely a straight rod ornamented at either end with a simple knob (Fig. 3).

He also gives a drawing of a violist of the fourteenth century, sculptured on the cathedral at Cologne, where the bow is even simpler in form. It is, however, impossible to judge how far the sculptor's imagination, or lack of observation, may have been responsible for these representations, so that they can hardly be taken as reliable evidence of the use of such primitive contrivances at so late a period.

CHAPTER II.

ORIENTAL ORIGIN OF THE BOW—INDIAN, CHINESE AND OTHER EASTERN BOWED INSTRUMENTS.

FIG. 4.

In attempting to trace the use of the bow to its source we are obliged to content ourselves with the generalized statement that it is undoubtedly of oriental origin. Thus, that it *had* an origin is proved beyond "all possible, probable shadow of doubt."

But whether the first form of bowed instrument became extinct prehistorically, or whether it still survives, as some suppose, in the Ravanastron of India, is not easily determined.

My own personal belief in the extreme antiquity of the bow is such as almost to justify the quaint statement of Jean Jacques Rousseau that Adam played the viol in Paradise.

Of existing bowed instruments the Ravanastron (Fig. 4) most certainly seems to be the oldest, as its structure is more primitive than any other.

Concerning this instrument legend runs to the effect that it was invented by Ravana, who was king of Ceylon some 5,000 years prior to the Christian era. How far this is accurate is impossible to say, for the oldest names for the bow known to Sanskrit scholars only take us back 1,500 to 2,000 years. Of these names it is interesting to note that the Kôna was evidently no more than a "friction rod" as, judging from the early descriptions, it would appear to have been without hair. Whether the Gârikâ or Parivàdas approached more nearly to the modern idea of a bow I am unfortunately not in a position to state with any degree of certainty.

The Ravanastron was, like the violin in its earliest stages, played only by the inferior classes of India; a fact that, as Engel clearly points out, makes it seem highly improbable that it was a Mohammedan importation, despite some writers' assertions to that effect. Undoubtedly it was introduced with Buddhism, from India into China, where it became modified in unimportant details into the Ur-heen.

A curious point in connection with some oriental fiddles, such as the Ur-heen, Uh-Ch'in (Fig. 5), Koka, etc., is that the hair of the bow passes between the strings.

FIG. 5.   FIG. 6.

Whether this circumstance is at all confirmatory of the supposition that the rod of the Trigonon was passed between the strings would be difficult to establish irrefutably; doubtless a logician could do so, but I prefer making a simple statement of facts rather than forcing them into agreement with any special theory; although I have plenty of worthy precedents for such a proceeding, for I have observed that most doubtful or disputed questions—the Bacon-Shakespeare controversy, for instance—are handled in this manner.

What strikes one very forcibly on looking into the use of the bow in the East is the great number of bowed instruments one finds. Thus in India we have the Ravanastron in various forms; the Omerti (Fig. 6), the Bengalese Sarindâ, etc.

In China, the Ur-heen, Uh-Ch'in, Saw-oo and Sawduang. In Siam, the Saw-tai, etc. In Turkey and Arabia, the Kemangeh-a-gouz (Fig. 7), Kemangeh-roumy, Rebâb-esh-Sha'er (Fig. 8), and Rebâb-el-maghanny, also the more modern Gunibry.

FIG. 7.   FIG. 8.

In Persia there is also an instrument strongly resembling the Omerti and Kemangeh in outline, called the Sitâra (Fig. 9). Then there is a primitive bowed instrument with three strings, known to the peasants of Russia as the Goudok, which is no doubt an immediate descendant of the three-stringed Rebâb, and, more remotely, of the Ravanastron. Abyssinia too, has its bowed instruments. In fact, the use of the bow is universal in the "glorious Orient," from whence nearly all products of western civilization are derived. In almost all cases great antiquity is ascribed to these instruments. The very name "Kemangeh-a-gouz," ancient in itself, can be roughly translated "ancient-fiddle," thus showing that the Persians [the name is Persian and bears out the Arab records that it came to them from Persia] considered it then a relic of the past, and that it was a survival of some still older instrument inherited, most likely from India. There can be little doubt that Fétis was right in assuming this to have been the Omerti, for, barring the long "tail-pin," the structure of both is almost identical.

FIG. 9.   FIG. 10.

The bows of all these instruments bear a strong resemblance to each other, as is only to be expected where all are of the simplest description. In the majority of cases the bow is merely a length of cane with a bunch of horse-hair tied at each end in such a manner as to pull the cane into a more or less pronounced curve. Those of the Goudok and Sarindâ (Fig. 10) are short, approach nearly to a semi-circle, and are quite rigid.

Those of the Ravanastron, Omerti, etc., are longer, and being more slender, have a certain amount of flexibility, but it does not appear that this latter qualification is sought for or considered indispensable. On the other hand, the now nearly obsolete Kokiu of Japan had a bow of about forty-five inches in length that was extremely elastic. It was made in sections after the manner of a fishing-rod, and the hair was tightened by the finger of the player, as in some of the early viol bows of Europe.

The method of hairing in most cases amounts to the simplest way of tying the hair on to the stick. Sometimes the hair is passed through a slit and held in place by a knot. In other specimens it is attached to a leather thong, and occasionally it is plugged into the open end of a piece of bamboo (Fig. 11).

FIG. 11.

The bows of the Saw-tai (Fig. 12), Uh-Ch'in, Koka and a few others show a distinct advance in point of curve and adjustment of hair, and strongly resemble the bow of the quaint Swedish Nyckelharpa in present use (Fig. 13).

FIG. 12.   FIG. 13.   FIG. 14.

The bows of the Sitâra (Fig. 9) and Saw-oo (Fig. 14), approach more nearly to the European form. The drawings of the latter, however, were made from highly ornate and elaborate specimens that may have been affected by Western influence. But against this must be set the religious conservatism of eastern nations. In many cases it would amount to gross sacrilege to alter in any way the construction of certain objects in daily use, so that we may take it generally that the east of to-day differs very little from what it was, even several thousand years ago, in such matters.

CHAPTER III.

THE CRWTH—FLEMING'S "ETRUSCAN RAVANASTRON"—
THE MEDIÆVAL BOW—UNRELIABILITY   OF EARLY DRAWINGS
AND SCULPTURES.

Perhaps the most interesting of the primitive bowed instruments is the Welsh Crwth. Unlike the still more ancient forms yet surviving in the East, it is now completely obsolete: unless we may count the Norwegian and Icelandic langspiel and fidla as descendants thereof.

At one time it was considered an ancestor of the violin, but since Mr. Heron-Allen brought his legal acumen and skill in sifting evidence to bear on the subject, we find that it must unquestionably be looked upon as the *last* of its race, and not as a direct forerunner of anything else. As to its origin, I should say it was two-fold. The oft-quoted lines of that seventh century Bishop, Venantius Fortunatus:—

"Romanusque lyra, plaudat tibi
Barbarus harpa
Græcus Achilliaca, Chrotta Britanna canat"

prove, however translated, that the Crwth was essentially British. The structure of the instrument strongly suggests its derivation from the Roman and Greek lyres, and I have little doubt that the first Crwth was in fact a lyre in the hands of one of our early British ancestors, who thought he would try thereon the effect of a Rebab or Kemangeh bow, and most probably got himself heartily laughed at for his pains. This is a kind of experiment that has been tried in modern times, as witness the "Streich-Guitarre" and more recent "Streich-Zither."

That the Eastern fiddles should have come to Britain then is not a very extravagant supposition. The distance is not great from northern Africa, through Spain, where a form of

Rebab is still played by the Basque peasantry, on through Europe generally and across the Channel to England. Also, it is very likely that there were a number of Orientals in attendance on the Imperial Court of the Cæsars who would naturally bring their customs, religions and arts with them.

I do not think the Greeks and Romans made any use of the bow whatever, although, considering the enormous spread of the Roman Empire, and, as I say, the diverse nationalities that surrounded the court, many of the Indian, Persian and African bowed instruments must have been fairly familiar objects in Rome and elsewhere. But being instruments of conquered nations; primitive in construction and strange in tonality; they were probably held in too light esteem ever to be adopted and developed by people of such importance and civilization as the Romans or Greeks.

I say all this with due respect to Mr. Fleming. This gentleman has contributed sundry valuable works to the bibliography of the violin, and in certain places mentions an Etruscan vase illustrated in a catalogue published by Prince Lucien Napoleon of Canino. He describes the decorations of this vase as follows: "The subject is a man seated reading a volume to two youths, who, leaning on knotted sticks, are listening attentively. On a little table or box in front of the principal figure is inscribed the name 'Chironeis.' On each side of the reader is an object which authorities in these matters term 'thecæ,' indicating the profession of this principal figure. One of these has a neck or handle, an oval disc, or sounding plane, and a tail piece extending below the disc rather more than half the length of the neck. From the upper extremity of the neck to the lower extremity of the disc are stretched strings, and across these strings at the centre of the disc is placed a bow of as rational construction as anything that has come down to us prior to the days of Corelli. The instrument is indeed almost identical with the Ravanastron." Now all this sounds very nice and extremely convincing, and whether or no Mr. Fleming himself believes the Greeks used the bow, I have no doubt that he is perfectly satisfied that he has proved such to be the case.

As I have seen neither the original vase or Prince Napoleon's catalogue, I feel some diffidence in throwing my half-ounce of doubt on this pound—good, thumping weight—of fact. However, I have seen the reproduction of the drawing as given by Mr. Fleming in his book, "Violins, Old and New," and, since he makes such a feature of this Grecian Ravanastron, I feel safe in assuming that it is accurately copied.

I distinctly remember first looking at that drawing. I gazed at it long and earnestly. I then referred to the text; after which I rapidly searched through the book to see if there was another drawing of a Greek vase. I thought perchance the printers in a playful mood might have transposed them; such things have happened. But it was not so; the drawing on page 250 was the only one. So I returned to it. There were the reader, the box, the inscription, the attentive youths with their knotted sticks, and, lastly, the "thecæ." I was not *long* in doubt as to which of these objects was the one Mr. Fleming attached so much importance to.

Ods catgut and fiddlesticks! as Bob Acres would genteelly have exclaimed. So this was the Etruscan Ravanastron I had dreamed about; this was the Greek fiddle I had discoursed so learnedly of when my pupils with childlike pertinacity questioned me as to the origin of the violin.

That is a useful sort of vase. If ever I come across anyone anxious to prove something, I shall advise him to use that drawing. That Ravanastron would prove anything; in fact it proved too much for me.

The more I have searched for pictorial records of bow in old prints and drawings, the more disappointed I have become. It is extraordinary how artists of genius have literally "scamped" the poor unfortunate "fiddle-stick" in such works. In the small room of prints and drawings at the British Museum is a drawing of a violinist attributed to Corregio. It is merely a slight sketch, but the violin is beautifully drawn; the corners are well expressed and the perspective is good, but the bow would be unrecognisable as such were it not for the close proximity of the violin. Even in more highly-finished productions the same thing obtains. I have found drawings of crowders, violists and fiddlers where every little detail of dimple, crease and nail has been almost photographically rendered in a hand holding what one knows must be a bow, but if the other hand held a shield, or a newspaper, or a child's whip-top would be accepted with equal readiness by the judicious observer as a sword, paper knife or whip respectively.

Occasionally one finds minute representations of bows, but these are more often than not of such a nature as to be impossible of credence as correct representations.

Another thing that stands in the way of a clear exposition of the bow's development is that even the most reliable drawings and sculptures do not show by any means a gradual improvement in the shape of the bow, for it is no uncommon thing to find fourteenth and fifteenth century representations of bows of quite eighth and ninth century type. It is not likely that any of such primitive bows would have remained in use unbroken for so many centuries, therefore I do not think these later representations of early bows can have been copied from actual specimens then in use, but, where not evolved from the artist's inner consciousness, may have been taken from the drawings, MSS., etc., handed down from the earlier periods. On this point Mr. Heron-Allen makes the following very sensible observations:—"The conclusion we are brought to is consequently this:*either* all representations of bows which have come down to us are unreliable, *or*, the bow, instead of developing as the fiddle undoubtedly did, remained in a state of primitive simplicity, and bore till a comparatively recent date the same relation to its companion the fiddle, as do the early specimens of Delft ware and the exquisite Sèvres specimens, which recline side by side in the cabinets of the delightfully incongruous nineteenth century drawing room. If you ask me to which of these conclusions I incline, I think the two deductions are to one another as three times two are to twice three, and that a combination of the two would probably account for the present misty aspect of the past history of the bow."

One should not lay too much stress on pictorial records; even our contemporary artists are not free from error, and it would be interesting to know what future writers on this subject will say of the nineteenth century violins and bows as represented by popular painters at the Royal Academy and other picture shows. They will find the evidence just as conflicting.

Unconvincing and contradictory as the existing records are, they are all we have, and, such as they are, I give a few selected examples.

A form of bow constantly occurring in drawings, etc., from the eighth to the sixteenth centuries, is Fig. 15. It is only slightly suggestive of the Oriental bows.

FIG. 15.   FIG. 16.   FIG. 17.

In the ninth century we find a bow (Fig. 16) strongly resembling those of the Saw-oo and Saw-Tai. And from the same century we find a miniature representation of a Crwth player with a bow slightly more distinctive in character (Fig. 17).

Similar bows to the above appear to have been pretty general in the tenth century. In the eleventh century a little more variety is apparent, as will be seen in Fig. 18.

FIG. 18.

Here are to be found the survival of the ninth century form shown in Fig. 17, and a remarkable advance in the form of the one at the bottom, which is doubtless the pattern intended to be shown in the sculptured bow, second from the top. The top one is merely given as an example of the perfunctory work the historian has to examine and yet retain his customary calm exterior.

Fig. 19 gives some examples of twelfth century bows as depicted by the artists of that period. The first two are evidently intended to represent the type shown in Fig. 17. The sculptor probably found the straight line of the hair inelegant. The third (which is from a MS. in the Bodleian Library) and last show a return to the ninth century form in Fig. 16.

FIG. 19.

This is a form that is found so continually through all the centuries, down to the seventeenth and eighteenth, that I am inclined to the belief that it is fairly accurate. It is very much like the outline of the modern double bass bow. In Fig. 20 are given some thirteenth century bows: the one with the curious sword-hilt is remarkable. In the others we find a return to more primitive lines.

FIG. 20.

The fourteenth century bows have very little to distinguish them from those of preceding ages, and I give the most noticeable examples I have found in Fig. 21. The second is a very advanced type. Against these must be set those in Fig. 22.

FIG. 21.

These appear to me as being most probably conventional representations, or copied from older works as suggested above.

FIG. 22.

Of fifteenth century bows, the pictorial and plastic arts record those shown in Fig. 23, together with the usual atavism or return to earlier types.

FIG. 23.

This atavism, if credible, is most marked in the sixteenth century as witness those in Fig. 24.

FIG. 24.

Here are bows that take us back to before the Norman Conquest, drawn by artists who were contemporary with Gasparo da Salo and Andreas Amati. It is quite out of the question to suppose that such bows were used at that time.

The drawings of seventeenth century bows are more convincing. We then get a more definite idea of the nut, which was in most cases a fixture. Also, the head begins to mould itself into something approaching the form of the modern "hatchet."

Although there are cases of bows in drawings as far back as the eleventh century (see Fig. 18, etc.) showing great advances, it is not until reaching the seventeenth century, that one can say with any degree of confidence that the perfect bow is on the horizon.

CHAPTER IV.

THE BEGINNINGS OF THE MODERN BOW—ORNAMENTATION—A POSSIBLE STRADIVARI BOW—THE MOVABLE NUT—THE CRÉMAILLÈRE—THE SCREWNUT.

I find it a matter for extreme regret that there should be such a large element of uncertainty in what I am able to bring forward of the earlier historical aspect of the bow. Of its primitive use one can do little more than examine contemporary evidence in the East, and then assume, albeit with some show of reason, that the same forms have survived from remote periods. Coming to the mediæval bow we appear to tread on safer ground; bows are depicted in miniatures, manuscripts, paintings, etc., from the eight and ninth centuries onwards, and in nearly every case we can determine the date of the production and frequently its author. So far nothing could be more satisfactory, but as I have said above, there are very few examples that impress one as being accurate representations.

Proceeding to the seventeenth and eighteenth centuries, I am further frustrated in my attempt to elucidate the obscure passages in the bow's history by a reversal of those conditions. I can now lay before my readers drawings and photographs of bows the accuracy of which I can guarantee, but placing them in perfect chronology is, unfortunately, little more than guess work. Such was the modesty of their makers that the early bows were all sent into the world nameless. Many of them are marvels of workmanship, and, though utterly unscientific in construction and unfit for the requirements of modern violinists, they are for the most part exquisite works of art upon which no pains have been spared.

Some of the fluting and other ornamentation is little short of marvellous in point of design and finish.

To a casual writer like myself the mass of conflicting detail found on examining ancient bows and the records of their use is extremely disconcerting. The practised scientist, however, surveys such things with calmness, for his trained eye immediately selects those details that support the theories he wishes to promulgate, and the rest are quietly consigned to oblivion.

In this way the most charmingly satisfactory results are obtained. Thus Fétis, in his article on Tourte, gives a brief outline of the history of the bow, illustrating the same with what purports to be a "*Display of the successive ameliorations of the bow in the seventeenth and eighteenth centuries.*" This consists of a series of drawings of bows ranging from Mersenne in 1620 through those used by Kircher, Castrovillari, Bassani, Corelli, Tartini and Cramer to that of Viotti in 1790. Herein is shown how the arched bow gave place to the straight: and this in its turn to that having the inward curve known as the "spring" or *cambre*. The succession is perfect, and it is only the final drawing of the series (the Viotti bow of 1790) that shows this *cambre*.

Now, in the collection of ancient bows kindly lent me by Mr. A. Hill for the purpose of illustrating these pages are several bows of a much earlier date, yet having the *cambre* most pronounced and, in some examples, extremely elegant.

Not being a scientist, I do not know how to omit these evidences of advance at such an early date from my writings on this subject, although I feel that by not doing so I am rendering this section of the work far from clear.

As a matter of fact clearness in what we can ascertain of the bow's history is a quality conspicuous by its absence; a condition doubtless due to the varying capacities of early bow makers, some of whom may have continued to make antiquated types whilst others of greater talent were anticipating in a measure the results of Tourte's genius and observation. It

has been observed in other branches of the world's progress that many have groped in the right direction for a space until there came one Genius who grasped, almost by intuition, the various requirements and produced the perfect work beyond which no man could go.

Entering upon the seventeenth century I now abandon the use of pictorial records of bows in favour of drawings and photographs made from actual specimens now in existence.

In Fig. 25 I give the heads of three remarkably interesting bows. I have drawn them the exact size of the originals. The first is most primitive throughout, though having an ingeniously contrived nut of which I shall speak more fully further on. The length of this bow is nearly 23 in.; the distance from the inside surface of the stick at the heel to the hair is ¾ in., and the width of the hair is ¼ in.

FIG. 25.

The second bow is extremely elegant, although useless as a bow: note the grace of the long peak. It is seldom that one finds these peaks so well preserved as many have been first broken and then cut down to remove the unsightly jagged end. The dimensions of this bow are:—Total length, 28¹/8 in.; length of hair, 23¼ in.; distance of hair from stick at heel, ¾ in.; breadth of hair ¼ in. The nut is on the same principle as the preceding one.

The third bow may be late seventeenth or early eighteenth century work. It is beautifully fluted throughout its entire length, the lower third having an extra raised line between the fluting. It is remarkable inasmuch as it has a movable nut working with a screw as in the modern bow and also a distinct *cambre*. The inward deviation of the stick from a straight line is a full quarter of an inch in 25½ in.; but this is too low down to give the bow a good spring. Being made, like the others in this figure, of that unyielding material snakewood, the experiment, though in the right direction, cannot be said to have been successful. The full length of this bow is 28½ in.; the length of the hair, 23½ in.

Plate I. is a photograph of an extremely interesting bow. Like the preceding example it has the conventional nut and *cambre*. In the matter of ornamentation it is probably unique. It is not only fluted throughout, but is inlaid with a minute mosaic of red, yellow and brown woods. In appearance it reminds one of the straw-work so popular at one period. Inlaid on one side of the nut are seen the Arms of Spain, and on the reverse is the Royal monogram. Mr. Alfred Hill procured this bow with some difficulty in Madrid and was able to trace its pedigree in so far as that it was originally with the instruments made by Stradivarius for the Spanish Court. There is just a shadow of possibility that it may be the actual work of that most glorious craftsman of Cremona.

PLATE. I.

Its length over all is 27½ in.; the playing length of the hair is 23¼ in.; the width of the hair barely ¼ in. This bow has the most scientific *cambre* as yet found. Its deviation is ⁹/16 in. in 26⁵/8 in. It is also of more flexible material than the others.

The centre bow in Fig. 26 is stamped by Thomas Smith (at last we have a signed specimen), chiefly known for his 'cellos. It was most probably made, however, by Edward Dodd. The head, while possessing a certain elegance, is of a very early type. It is of yellow lance wood and has a very pronounced *cambre*, the deviation being nearly ½ in. in 27¼ in. The total length is 28¾ in., and from the mortices in the head and nut one would suppose that it was intended to take somewhat broader hair than the preceding examples. The date of the bow is somewhere between 1760 and 1780. The other bows in Fig. 26 are viola da gamba bows; the upper one I use frequently myself in certain pieces for that instrument. It is very elegant and I should say is of French make. It is extremely flexible and most adapted to sustaining chords of three notes, as the great distance of the hair from the stick prevents any "grinding" on the middle string. But like all these early bows the hair is much too narrow.

The other gamba bow in Fig. 26 is very quaint and appears to be of much earlier date. It is handsomely fluted through the upper two thirds: the lower third being a simple octagonal. A curious feature is that the distance of the hair from the stick gradually diminishes from 1 in. at the heel to ½ in. at the point. It has a slight *cambre*, but being of snake wood is quite poker-like in its rigidity.

FIG. 26.

As is it impossible to determine the exact date of these bows, one can arrive at no very safe conclusion as to when the movable nut was first introduced. Fétis thinks this important modification came from the East also, and he mentions a cherry wood bow in his possession, made at Bagdad, which has a distinct head where the hair is inserted, and a nut fitting into a dovetail notch in the stick.

The first and second of the bows shown in Fig. 25 have a curious device. The hair is fixed into the stick at both ends, and the nut, which is quite detached, slips into a slot with a snap, and is held in place by the pressure of the hair. A glance at Fig. 27 will make this arrangement clear. These two nuts are the second and third in Fig. 28, which is reduced one-third below actual size. The ornamental tip to the middle one looks as though it had a screw, but this is merely a decoration to balance a finely fluted design on the stick just above where the "lapping" is usually placed.

FIG. 27.   FIG. 28.

A great advance on this was the *crémaillère* (Fig. 29), which served to vary the tension of the hair in a more or less satisfactory manner. This device is still in use in Sweden.

FIG. 29.

The actual invention of the movable nut travelling on a propelling and withdrawing screw is attributed to the elder Tourte, but some of the bows in Mr. Hill's collection having this contrivance appear to be too remote for this to be the case. It is a point that I fear will always be shrouded in mystery.

PLATE. II.

In Plate II. we see a nearer approach to the outlines of the modern bow. These I should say are the work of W. Tubbs, who worked for most of the English fiddle makers and dealers. The first one bears the stamp of Norris and Barnes. This bow is $27^{7}/8$ in. in length, the other two being exactly one inch longer. The hair in the first and third is ¼ in. in width; in the centre one it is full $5/16$ in. The handsome ivory nut of this bow is shown in Fig. 28. They are extremely elegant, and have much of the character of the modern bow in finish and *cambre*, though the deviation is again too low down.

CHAPTER V.

VUILLAUME'S FACTS—THE FERRULE AND SLIDE—JOHN DODD.

Another example of bow, remarkable not only for its ornamentation, but also as having a well defined *cambre* together with a nut and screw, is Fig. 30.

FIG. 30.

This is a Cremonese bow of the seventeenth century. It is fluted in alternate sections, or panels, the lower third having a slight extra complication of the design "thrown in." Truly these grand old craftsmen were not afraid of work. The screw-nut is as perfect as one could wish, saving, only, in the meagre allowance of hair provided for.

These early bows with screw-nuts quite dispel the generally accepted theory that this mechanical contrivance for regulating the tension and preserving the elasticity of the stick was the invention of the elder Tourte. The majority of writers on the history of the violin, and, incidentally, the bow, are content to take their data from that much quoted historian and scientist, Fétis. He appears to have made most of his more important statements on the authority of Vuillaume. How Vuillaume became so versed in the history of his craft does not appear. His talent in the way of producing "genuine" Cremonese and other masterpieces is well known, the most stupendous example being the Duiffoprugcar instruments with which he imposed on the violin world so successfully. May we infer that he had equal facility in the fabrication of historical "facts"? *De mortuis nil nisi bonum,* but at all cost our history must be made accurate. Better no facts at all than spurious ones.

Having disposed of the screw attachment, the next important points in the development of the bow is the ferrule, which preserves the ribbon-like appearance of the hair, and the slide, which serves as an ornamental cover for the mortice in which the hair is fixed. These additions are commonly attributed to François Tourte, but in Fig. 31 I give a drawing of a typical nut by John Dodd, having both these improvements.

FIG. 31.

Dodd and Tourte were contemporaries, Tourte's birth having taken place only five years before that of Dodd in 1752. When I come to speak more particularly of Tourte I shall show my reasons for thinking it unlikely that Dodd copied Tourte in this respect. The whole matter is shrouded in mystery. In other branches of science, art, etc., we find brilliant thinkers arriving simultaneously at identical results,* and I can quite believe that the idea of the ferrule and slide (obvious contrivances when one considers the requirements of a good bow) could have occurred to more than one of the workers then striving after perfection.

* As a noteworthy example, take the simultaneous discovery by deduction of the invisible planet Neptune, by Adams and Leverrier.

The characteristic feature I wish to call attention to in the heel shown above (Fig. 31) is the great size of the slide in proportion to the whole lower surface of the nut. It leaves such a very small margin compared with that of other makers. This will be found in nearly every genuine specimen. Unfortunately nuts wear out and become replaced with new ones, so that it is not always possible to obtain a bow that is original in all its parts. Dodd occasionally decorated the face of his bows with mother-of-pearl, as in the example shown in Fig. 31. He invariably stamped the name DODD in large, plain letters both on the side of the nut and on the stick. I have seen some that are stamped J. Dodd, but not many. Fig. 32

shows (actual size) a very early Dodd head, than which nothing, I think, could be more distressingly ugly. It is remarkable that such a caricature should have emanated from the same man who produced those shown in Plates III. and IV. Plate III. consists of photographs (actual size) of two violin bows, and one tenor bow, Plate IV. giving one tenor bow and one 'cello bow by this maker. It would be quite impossible to give representations of all Dodd's characteristics, as his work varies so very much. I have therefore chosen a few only of the best types. These are all exceptionally well finished. In the second and third is to be seen the tendency to arch in the neck of the bow so frequent in Dodds; in the others the sweep of the stick up to the head is perfect. His 'cello bows are his best work, and compare favourably with the greatest Continental makers. The one I have selected is of the finest period. The first of the two tenor bows (third on Plate III.) is the type of head most frequently seen, some have the head drawn backward at a very ungainly angle, and others, again, slope forwards, to an extent greater even than that of the 'cello bow in Plate IV.

FIG. 32.

PLATE. III.

PLATE. IV.

Owing to the extreme elegance of Dodd's bows, and the beautiful workmanship of his finest specimens, he has been dubbed the "English Tourte," and amongst the majority of English amateurs the name of Dodd is held in the highest possible estimation. But as a matter of fact very few Dodd bows are worthy of this regard. His best bows, such as he sold for a pound or thirty shillings, are fine, although few of the violin bows are such as an artist would make much use of. The slenderness is frequently carried to excess, and the narrowness of the head prevents a sufficient "spread" being given to the hair in many cases, and a great number are much too short.

It must be remembered that Dodd worked before foreign importation annihilated the English violin and bow making industries, and he turned out a large number of bows at prices ranging from a few shillings a dozen upwards. Thus it will be readily understood that there are many genuine Dodds in existence that are not worth looking at. His tenor bows are often excellent, and, as I said above, his 'cello bows represent him the best.

CHAPTER VI.

DR. SELLÈ'S RECOLLECTIONS OF DODD—HIS WORK AND POVERTY—DODD ANDTOURTE—THE CALCULATION OF FÉTIS AND VUILLAUME.

It has been my great good fortune to be favoured with an interview with the veteran violinist, Doctor Sellè, of Richmond. This gentleman, now well on in his eighties, knew John Dodd most intimately, and gave me many interesting details about him. I have endeavoured to obtain a portrait of Dodd, but there does not seem to be anything of the sort in existence. However, Dr. Sellè gave me a graphic description of his personal appearance. In stature he was short and of a shuffling gait. As he affected nether garments of extreme brevity, very broad-brimmed hats, and was excessively negligent in the matter of clothing, etc., his habitual aspect was quaint and eccentric to a degree.

He was unfortunately very illiterate, and, according to Dr. Sellè, it is doubtful whether he could sign his own name.

In his work—the artistic excellence of which is remarkable under these circumstances—he was very secretive, giving as his reason for taking no apprentice, his desire that no one else should ever know or perpetuate his methods.

It has been said, and, I believe, on good authority, that he was once offered the sum of £1,000 for his "secret," a temptation that, despite his great poverty, he steadfastly resisted.

Doctor Sellè tells me that he distinctly remembers seeing Dodd cut out a bow from the rough plank with a curiously constructed double saw.

This is very remarkable as none of the bow makers now working know of such a tool, or can conceive the possibility of using one. Whether this may have any connexion with the much talked of "secret," it is impossible to say. It is probably another of those points in the history of the bow that seem doomed to remain shrouded in mystery.

Doctor Sellè remembers seeing Dodd walking home many times with his pockets full of oyster shells begged from various stalls.

From these he used to cut out the pearl for the slides and ornamentation on his bows. This accounts for the characteristic plainness of these features of his work. He was often at a loss for silver for the mountings, and the Doctor says it was highly diverting to him when a boy to hear the old housekeeper soundly rating Dodd for melting down *another* of her metal spoons.

One great drawback to Dodd's success was his partiality for the "flowing bowl." As the Doctor epigramatically expressed it in the notes he supplied to A. Vidal, "he was very regular in his irregularities." Vidal's translation at this point is worthy of note. One is surprised to find that Dodd would pay four daily visits to "les voitures et chevaux publics"—"the public carriages and horses."

The mind fails to grasp the Gallic conception of the eccentric Englishman whose nationally characteristic love of horseflesh should cause him so frequently to inspect the omnibus of the period.

One shudders to think what Vidal would have done if Dodd's favourite house of call had been the Star and Garter instead of the *Coach and Horses!*

His last years were spent in great poverty; in fact, he subsisted almost entirely on the charity of a few violinists and amateurs who appreciated his genius. He ultimately died of bronchitis in the Infirmary of Richmond Workhouse, and was buried at Kew; not, as has been elsewhere stated, at Richmond.

I do not think a man of such a taciturn, secretive disposition, would have been likely readily to adopt the methods and copy the work of another maker. As has been shown by the reproductions of bows I have given so far, there has been apparent a converging tendency to the modern design of head all through. The Tourte head is undoubtedly the most beautiful, the most perfect in every way. His was the master hand that *did* what others had been trying to do. Dodd, working, as I believe, quite independently, came very near it. A comparison of the Dodd bows shown in Plates III. and IV., with the Tourtes in Plates V. and VI., will make clear a very significant fact. Dodd's work—fine as it is—is distinctly *earlier* in spirit than that of his great French rival. Yet they were contemporaries—in point of fact Dodd was a few years later than Tourte.

PLATE. V.

PLATE. VI.

Then, as regards the *cambre*, Dodd followed on in the primitive school and cut his bows at once to the required sweep: Tourte, in addition to perfecting the dimensions and design, instituted an entirely new principle based on scientific deductions. His bows were all cut straight, and the "spring" was produced by judicious heating of the fibres.

Another thing one has to consider in this connexion is the relations that existed between England and France at this period. I think most people will admit that they were "strained," and that there were many obstacles in the way of free intercourse between the two countries. The war with France commenced when Dodd was twenty-one years of age, and though Tourte was five years older he had spent his youth firstly in the pursuit of a vocation entirely removed from bow making, and secondly in experiments lasting some considerable time before he commenced producing the perfect work that has made his name one to be extolled and reverenced by all wielders of that magic wand, the "fiddle-stick." When one thinks of the roundabout way such a thing would have to travel from Paris to London at this period, it seems highly probable that Dodd may not have seen a specimen of Tourte's work until he was about sixty.

What a marvellous thing a fine Tourte is! What a revelation the first time a player handles one! When I have an opportunity of playing on a Strad with a Tourte I can never decide which causes me the most delight. There is an indefinable something about a Tourte that seems to increase the player's dexterity of manipulation to an extraordinary extent. No matter how used one may be to a certain bow: no matter how expert one may be in the execution of staccato and arpeggio passages, the first time a Tourte is tried one realizes that hitherto there has been an effort necessary for the adequate production of such effects, whereas now the bow seems endowed with a consciousness quite *en rapport* with that of the player, and difficulties vanish magically. It seems voluntarily to carry into effect the player's wishes without any physical interposition whatever.

It is like riding a thoroughbred in the "Row" after driving a donkey across Hampstead Heath. Not that I or any of my readers would think of indulging in any such distressingly vulgar exercise as the last named. It may serve, however, to conjure up in the mind a sufficiently forcible simile.

Apart from their many wonderful qualities as bows, they are quite exceptional as works of art. Study the four heads shown in Plates V. and VI., and note the tender sweep of the outer line; full of force and delicacy combined. See, too, how it is supported by the harmonious inner line, a thought more rigid, and yet full of grace. To become an expert in bows requires years of continual observation, for the slight differences in line are too subtle to be apparent to those who are not constantly looking for and studying them. But I think anyone, even "ye meanest capacitie in ye world"—to quote good old Roger North—will be able to appreciate the contrast between the bow heads in Plates III. and IV., and those in Plates V. and VI. It is in the two 'cello bow heads that the greatest resemblance is seen. But even here one can easily note the unwonted massiveness, almost amounting to clumsiness, in that of Dodd; while the Tourte is full of lightness, strength and vigour. There is more or less of sluggishness observable in most of the preceding bows, but the Tourte is *awake;* it lives!

It is at times of great interest to note by what slender threads of chance great consequences may be suspended. Take the family of the Tourtes for instance. We find the father a worthy craftsman making bows as good, and possibly better, than those of his contemporaries. He, obeying a natural law of custom, educated his eldest son in his own craft, and probably looked to him to perpetuate those excellencies in design and finish that had brought him fame. François, the younger son, was not forgotten though, and the father bethought him of some useful industry at which he might earn a living, and decided on clockmaking as the most suitable. Now mark the erratic workings of fate. The eldest son, from whom so much was expected, proved a comparative failure, inasmuch as that, instead of progressing, his work was distinctly inferior to that of his father.* François, on the other hand, became tired of clockmaking after eight years' ill-remunerated grind, and turned his attention to the family trade.

* The few fine bows by "Tourte-l'aîné," as he was called, I should think were made after his brother's success in this direction.

He, like Dodd, was totally uneducated, but had great gifts of perception and judgment.

At this time violin playing was becoming every day more distinctive and prominent. Great players were beginning to understand the *chiar oscuro* of music. They were learning expression.

There was in general amongst violinists an anticipation of the grand, yet simple law set forth by De Beriot in his Violin School that the human voice was the pure archetype upon which all *played* music should be modelled.

It was found that the violin was capable of simulating all the subtle inflexions of song, whether of passion or tenderness, and players sighed for an ideal bow that should be tongue-like in its response to the performer's emotion. A bow that should at once be flexible to "whisper soft nothings in my lady's ear"; strong—to sound a clarion-blast of defiance; and, withal, be ready for any *coquetterie* or *badinage* that might suit its owner's whim. This is what François Tourte, the starving clockmaker, gave them.

We fiddlers have to be very thankful that the master clockmakers of Paris were not more liberal to their employés!

Illiterate as he was he at once grasped all the points of art and physics involved, and commenced diligently experimenting with a view to solving the various problems that presented themselves to his consideration.

To gain facility in the manipulation of his tools, he made countless bows from old barrel staves; he could not afford to make his first attempts on anything better. When he had attained sufficient skill in the actual workmanship, and had satisfied himself as to the most suitable form, he set to work investigating the question of material. He tried all kinds of wood, and at last decided that the red wood of Pernambuco, then largely imported into Europe for dyeing purposes, was the best. To obtain this in sufficient quantities was no easy matter, for the Anglo-French wars were interfering seriously with international commerce; a circumstance that rendered this material unusually expensive. Then the nature of this wood is not by any means a bow maker's ideal. Billets and logs amounting to several tons in weight may be examined before a piece is found sufficiently free from knots and cracks, and of straight enough grain to be suitable for the purpose. However, genius *and* a capacity for taking infinite pains overcame all difficulties, and we now have bows worthy of the greatest masterpieces of Cremona.

How little are the workings of genius understood by the "painstaking" ones. They cannot conceive the suddenness of inspiration—the almost instantaneous grasp of essentials that precedes the plodding mechanical work necessary even to genius.

The results of "infinite pains," or of genius alone are equally unsatisfactory. It is only where these qualities are combined in perfect balance that true greatness can be achieved.

In the case of Tourte we have a remarkable example of this combination. His genius made him grasp spontaneously the qualities required, and his capacity for taking infinite pains helped him to produce the perfect bow. He it was who determined finally the length and weight of a bow, its equilibrium, the angle of the hair necessary for a good "attack," the length and breadth of the hair and sundry other points that, prior to 1775, had been quite undecided.

The mean length of a violin bow as fixed by Tourte is from 74 to 75 centimètres (29.134 to 29.528 inches English); that of a viola bow is 74 centimètres (29.134 inches), and a 'cello bow 72 to 73 centimètres (28.347 to 28.740). Many people imagine that the plates of silver or gold with which the nut of a bow is inlaid are nothing more than mere ornamentation. But their first purpose is distinctly one of utility, which is as it should be in a work of art; superfluous decoration has no beauty for an artist. It is by means of these metal "loadings" at the heel that the weight of the head is counteracted and the exact point of equilibrium determined. The centre of gravity in a violin bow should be at 19 centimètres (7.48 inches) from the nut; in a 'cello bow at 175 to 180 millimètres (6.89 to 7.087 inches) from the nut.

Concerning the geometric proportions of the Tourte bows, I cannot do better than quote Bishop's able translation of the explanation given by Fétis in his notice of A. Stradivarius.

"The medium length of a bow, to the head exclusively, is 0^m, 700 (27.56 inches).

"The bow comprises a cylindrical or prismatic part of uniform dimensions, the length of which is 0^m, 110 (4.33 inches). When this portion is cylindrical, its diameter is 0^m, $008^6/10$ (.34 inch).

"From this cylindrical or prismatic portion the diameter of the bow decreases up to the head, where it is reduced to 0^m, $005^3/10$ (.21 inches). This gives a difference of 0^m, $003^3/10$ of a millimètre (.13 inch) between the diameters of the extremities; from whence it follows that the stick comprises ten points where its diameter is necessarily reduced by $3/10$ of a millimètre (.012 inch) reckoning from the cylindrical portion.

FIG. 33.

"After proving by a great number of Tourte's bows that these ten points are not only found always at decreasing distances on the same stick, but also that the distances are perceptibly the same, and that the situations of the points are identical on different bows compared together, M. Vuillaume sought to ascertain whether the positions of the ten points could not be obtained by a geometrical construction, by which they might be found with certainty; and by which, consequently, bows might be made whose good condition should be always settled *à priori*. This he attained in the following manner. At the extremity of a right line A B, equal to 0^m, 700 (27.56 inches), that is to say the length of the bow, raise a perpendicular A C, equal to the length of the cylindrical portion, namely 0^m, 110 (4.33 inches).

"At the extremity B of the same line, raise another perpendicular B D, of the length 0^m, 022 (.866 inches) and unite the upper extremities of these two perpendiculars, or ordinates by a right line C D, so that the two lines A B and C D, may lie at a certain inclination to each other.

"Take the length 0^m, 110 (4.33 inches) of the ordinate A C with the compasses, and set it off on the line A B, from A to *e:* from the point thus obtained, draw another ordinate (parallel to A C and perpendicular to A B), until it meets the line C D.

"Between these two ordinates A C and *e f*—the latter of which is necessarily less than the former—lies the cylindrical portion of the bow, whose diameter, as before stated, is 0^m, $008^6/10$ (.34 inch).

"Then take the length of the ordinate last obtained, *e f*, and set it off, as before, on the line A B, from *f* to *g*, and at the point *g* draw a third ordinate *g h*, the length of which must also be set off on the line A B, to determine thereon a new point *i*, from which to draw the fourth ordinate, *i j*: the length of which, likewise, when set off on the line A B, determines the point where the fifth ordinate *k l* is to be drawn. The latter, in like manner, determines the sixth *m n*, and so of the others, to the last but one *y z*.

"The points *g i k m o q s u w y* so obtained, starting from the point *e*, are those where the diameter of the bow is successively reduced $3/10$ of a millimètre (.012 inch). Now, these points have been determined by the successively decreasing lengths of the ordinates drawn from the same points, and their respective distances progressively decrease from the point *e* to the point B.

"If we subject these data to calculation, we shall find that the profile of the bow is represented by a logarithmic curve, of which the ordinates increase in arithmetical progression; while the abscissæ increase in geometrical progression; and lastly, that the curvature of the profile will be expressed by the equation

$$y = -3.11 + 2, 57 \log. x;$$

and, in varying x from 175 to 165 tenths of a millimètre, the corresponding values of y will be those of the radii (or semi-diameters) of the transverse circular section of the bow at corresponding points in the axis."

CHAPTER VII.

LUPOT—PECCATTE—SPURIOUS STAMPING—PANORMO—W. J. B. WOOLHOUSE'S CALCULATIONS.

I have spoken at length of Dodd and Tourte—two names that stand out in the history of the bow with remarkable prominence—and before proceeding with the general list of bow makers, great and small, I propose to speak of Peccatte and Lupot, whose genius was inferior only to that of Tourte in that they were followers rather than originators.

François Lupot was a brother of Nicolas Lupot the violin maker. He, however, devoted all his energies to the manufacture of bows, and, in his best work, is considered by many to nearly equal Tourte. But unfortunately the standard of excellence in Lupot's bows varies to a considerable extent, and, while some are truly magnificent others are very inferior. This is a fact that cannot be too widely made known in the interests of intending purchasers. The guarantee of genuineness alone is not sufficient for anyone desiring a bow for use, and, unless he has the requisite knowledge and experience himself he should always first submit a bow to a professional man of repute for his judgment as to its qualities for a player. Many of Lupot's sticks are stamped "LUPOT," sometimes in two or three places, but it has been doubted whether he did this himself or not. In general it is thought that it was done afterwards by dealers. This is certainly the case with the few Tourtes that are stamped with their maker's name, for it is an ascertained fact that the Tourtes never stamped their work. There are only two instances on record of Tourte marking a stick, and in each case it consisted of a minute label glued into the slot bearing the following inscription: "Cet archet a été fait par Tourte en 1824, âge de soixante-dix-sept ans." (This bow was made by Tourte in 1824, aged 77 years).

An important addition, said to have been instituted by Lupot, was the metal plate which lines the groove in the nut and prevents the wearing away of the nut by friction with the stick.

In Plate VII. I give two examples of Lupot's work. Here will be seen all the tenderness of line characteristic of Tourte, albeit that they lack somewhat of his force. The workmanship in these two bows is superb, and they are also delightful to play with, being well balanced and of controllable flexibility. This is a point in a bow that is frequently overlooked. Many imagine that flexibility alone is the chief desideratum, and bows have been shown to me almost indiarubber-like in their pliancy; the owners expecting me to wax enthusiastic over this—to my mind—serious defect. As a matter of fact, flexibility and pliancy are not correct definitions of a bow's chief quality, as they amount to weakness. What is really meant is elasticity, by which is conveyed not only the property of yielding to pressure but also that of speedily recovering its normal state. We sometimes hear a player in testing bows say that such a one has too much "life" in it; thereby implying that its action is largely out of the performer's control, a condition usually attributable to an excess of flexibility.

PLATE. VII.

As a contrast to the Lupot bows in Plate VII., I give two examples of Dominique Peccatte, Plate VIII. Here we have forcibleness and energy to a most marked extent, yet there is a certain grace withal, the extreme squareness of the outer line does not offend the eye as in those of Dodd.

PLATE. VIII.

Peccatte, like François Tourte, started life in an occupation far removed from that which made him famous. His father was a barber at Mirecourt, where Dominique was born 1810. Wielding the razor not proving congenial, he adopted the prevailing industry of the town and became a maker of violins and bows; in the latter he became exceptionally expert. In the year 1826 J. B. Vuillaume was in want of a talented workman and wrote to his brother, who was established in Mirecourt, to find him one. The result of these enquiries was that Dominique Peccatte came to Paris and remained for eleven years with Vuillaume. In 1837 François Lupot died and Peccatte took over the business. Ten years later he returned to his native place, though retaining his business connexion with Paris until his death, which took place in 1874. Many of his bows are unstamped, or bear the stamp of Vuillaume, but great numbers of them are stamped "PECCATTE," occasionally with the word "PARIS" on the opposite side of the stick.

Much confusion has arisen from the fact that in some specimens the stamp has only a single "T," the result, probably, of illiteracy on the part of the maker.

The third in Plate VIII. is a bow by Panormo. His work is quite distinct from that of any other maker; but one must not run away with the idea that he affected an unjustifiable singularity, for the flat sides and angular facets of the Panormo heads have a logical basis, being in point of fact the natural continuation of the octagonal stick.

Indebted as we are to the makers and scientists of France for bringing the indispensable "fiddlestick" to such a degree of perfection, we must not overlook the claims of certain of our own countrymen for recognition in the same field of art.

The late mathematician and musical amateur, W. S. B. Woolhouse, no less than Fétis, contributed greatly to a full understanding of the essential properties of a bow on the part of those whose office it is to produce the actual instrument. Woolhouse laid great stress on a point overlooked by many other students of the subject, the same being that the success of a bow depends quite as much on its purity as a vibrating body as does the violin.

Unless the bow is so adjusted in its weight and proportions that it vibrates with absolute uniformity throughout its entire length it is useless to an artist.

Bows are "false" frequently in the same way that strings are. Inequalities of finish, imperceptible to our ordinary senses, will render a perfect "*staccato*" from end to end impossible, just as it is impossible to obtain true fifths in every part of a violin's compass if one of the strings be slightly wanting in absolute cylindricity. I speak specially of "*staccato*," as that form of bowing suffers perhaps more than any other from faulty bows; but any form of bowing that calls for special dexterity will betray the inefficiency of a bow.

It is of great interest to compare the calculations of Woolhouse with those of Fétis, and I will here quote the results obtained by the former.

"If measurements be taken in inches, and parts of an inch, and h denote the distance of any part of the bow from the head, the diameter of the stick in that locality, supposing the bow to be round, may be readily calculated from the following formula:—

$$\text{Diameter} = .2\,[\log.(h + 7.25) - 9.8100]$$

"From this formula the numbers given in the last column of the following table were calculated."

	Distance from Head of Bow in Inches.		
Violin	Viola	Violoncello	Diameter in parts of an inch.
0			.210
2	0		.230
4	1½	0	.247
6	3	1	.262
9	5	3	.280
13	8	5½	.300
18	11½	9	.318
23	15	12	.333
	19	16	.348
	23	20	.360
		24	.370

These measurements, of course, only extend to the commencement of the cylindrical portion.

Woolhouse made a small gauge of ivory, based on the above measurements, which proved of great practical value in examining bows. The measurements he obtained by the above calculation apply to wood of medium density. He says, "For close and dense wood the dimensions should be somewhat diminished, or, what amounts practically to the same thing, the distance from the head should, for dense wood, be increased by half an inch, or an inch, as the case may be, before applying the gauge." He then gives a table of inclusive weights of violin, viola and violoncello bows.

	Weight of Bow for		
	Violin	Viola	Violoncello
Light	grains	grains	grains
Medium	850	1,000	1,150
Heavy	900	1,050	1,200
	950	1,100	1,250

In speaking of the adjustment of the spring or *cambre*, Woolhouse gives a means of obtaining the exact curve that does not strike me as being sufficiently reliable for the purpose. He suggests that "an auxiliary bow be made of the proper dimensions, but so as to be quite straight; then, on being haired and screwed up in the ordinary way, it will show, in an inverted position, the exact curve to which other bows should be set." But "screwed up in the ordinary way" appears to me to admit of too much latitude of application: it is not possible to divine to what extent this auxiliary bow *is* to be screwed, and if *this* is left to the judgment of the maker, why not set the *cambre* by judgment and save the trouble of the straight auxiliary bow?

I will now proceed to give an alphabetical list of bow makers which I trust is as complete as possible. I have endeavoured to leave out all purely factory makers in favour of those who are personally engaged in the manufacture of bows. There are some in the list who are not actual makers, but who carefully supervise all the bows issued under their name. Such work is always distinctive and differs greatly from that issued by firms who order bows by the gross from foreign factories, and then stamp their own name on the stick. This is a class of bow that usually looks very pretty and tempting to the young lady amateur, but is sadly lacking in balance and spring; what little there may be of the latter at first soon disappears, for it is quite impossible for any firm to turn out thoroughly efficient bows at the extraordinarily low prices one sees quoted. One must remember that for a bow to be of any real utility, the material, the workmanship, and the fittings must be of the very best possible description.

CHAPTER VIII.

A LIST OF BOW MAKERS.

A noticeable feature in the following list is the great preponderance of French makers. Curiously enough the list of bow makers commences with:

ADAM, JEAN DOMINIQUE. He was born at Mirecourt in 1795, and died at the age of sixty-nine. He is said by some to have been the son of one Jean Adams, a bow maker of the eighteenth century. How far this may be true is impossible to say. The difference in the spelling of the name may not be a great matter, but there is no explanation forthcoming. The majority of his bows are very commonplace, but occasionally he "made an effort" and produced something out of his ordinary run, and these he invariably stamped ADAM. Of these the octagonal sticks are most highly prized.

ALLEN, SAMUEL. Born in Cornwall in 1858; was originally intended for a schoolmaster. Worked at several mechanical trades and being musical, he naturally turned his attention to fiddles, and ultimately, bows. Messrs. W. E. Hill and Sons employed him as a bow maker for several years. Although he held a high position in their workshop his independent nature was not satisfied until 1891, when he set up in business on his own account as a violin and bow maker and repairer.

BAROUX, Paris. Early half of the present century. Occasionally made some very excellent bows, but the general average of his work is only moderate.

BAUSCH AND SON, Leipsic. Middle of present century. The bows issued by this firm are valued highly in Germany. They are well made and, as a rule, strong.

BAZIN, GUSTAVE, Mirecourt. A very capable workman, some of his 'cello bows are excellent.

BETTS. Born 1755, died 1823. Worked in London as a violin maker and dealer. The bows bearing his name were made by Edward Dodd and W. Tubbs.

BRAGLIA, ANTONIO, Modena. Beginning of this century. I have not seen any of this maker's work.

BROWN, JAMES (Junior), London. Born 1786, died 1860. A clever maker, worked much for the trade, but turned out some good sticks, stamped with his name.

CHANOT, ADOLPH, Paris. Brother of the late Georges Chanot of Wardour Street. Born about 1828. Worked with Henry of Paris and has turned out some magnificent sticks. His death, which took place suddenly, at the age of twenty-nine, was due to an aneurism. Had he lived he would undoubtedly have taken a high position in the esteem of bow wielders.

DARBEY, GEORGE, Bristol. Died March, 1921.

DODD, EDWARD, London and Sheffield. Born 1705, died 1810. One seldom finds a bow bearing his name as he was mostly employed by others, such as Betts, Forster, Norris, etc.

DODD, JAMES. Worked in London in 1864; it is doubtful if any of his work can be identified as he almost invariably worked for others.

DODD, JOHN. Born in 1752, died in 1839. This was *the* English bow-maker *par excellence*. For fuller details of his life and work see Chapter VI."

DODD, THOMAS, London, 1786-1823. He differed from the others of this name inasmuch as he did not make for others but employed others to make for him.

EURY, Paris. Early part of the present century. His bows are universally esteemed, some of them being exceptionally fine. He did not always stamp his bows, but when he did it was generally under the "lapping" or, as some say, the "whipping."

FONCLAUSE, JOSEPH. Born in 1800, died in 1865. He was an excellent maker. He first learnt the art of bow-making from Pajeot at Mirecourt, and ultimately worked for J. B. Vuillaume at Paris. Later on he started on his own account. His bows from this period are usually marked with his own name.

FORSTER, WILLIAM. A noted English violin maker who was born near the middle of the last century. One now and then meets with a bow bearing his name. These are all the work of E. Dodd, W. Tubbs, or some other skilled workmen in his employ.

GAND AND BERNARDEL, Paris. A modern firm whose staff make some remarkably fine bows. They are mostly stamped with the name of the firm; but as they make bows to the order of various other firms there are many examples of their work either unstamped or bearing fictitious names.

HARMAND. Worked in Mirecourt about 1835. Made some fairly good bows.

HENRY. Born in 1812 at Mirecourt where he first learnt his craft. He worked there till his twenty-fifth year, when he went to Paris. Here he was employed by Chanot first, and later, by Peccatte. When Peccatte left Paris, Henry entered into partnership with Simon, another workman in Peccatte's employ who had succeeded to the latter's Paris shop. This partnership lasted till 1851. He then worked alone. He was a magnificent workman and has produced some splendid bows. I have in mind a 'cello bow of his shown me by J. Chanot that is a marvel of strength and elasticity. He died in 1870. Sometimes his bows are stamped "Henry, Paris."

HILL, W. E., AND SONS, London. Contemporary. This firm issue some very fine bows which are made in their own workshops by expert workmen trained under the personal supervision of Mr. A. Hill.

JOSEPHS. American, contemporary. A very clever maker and repairer of violins and bows. I have seen some of his work that was excellent.

KITTEL, St. Petersburg. Modern. I have never come across a specimen of this maker's work. Fleming states that they "are about as nearly equal to Tourte's as those of any maker that has lived since his day." It is a pity they are not more plentiful if this is the case.

KNOPF, HEINRICH, and KNOPF, LUDWIG, Berlin, contemporary. Fairly good bows made chiefly to the order of other firms.

LAFLEUR, JACQUES. Born at Nancy in 1760, died in Paris 1832. One of the best of the old makers. Some continental authorities place him on a par with Tourte. Those of his make that I have handled are certainly very fine indeed.

LAFLEUR, JOSEPH RENÉ, Paris. Born in 1812, died in 1874. He was the son of Jacques Lafleur and inherited much of his father's skill.

LAMY, ALFRED JOSEPH. Born in 1850 at Mirecourt. He was an excellent maker. An interesting feature is that he learnt his craft at a remarkably early age. He worked first with Gautrot at Chateau-Fleurry. He went, like the rest, to Paris in 1877, and worked for Voirin for some eight years. At Voirin's death he started in business for himself.

LUPOT, FRANÇOIS. Born at Orleans 1774, died at Paris in 1837. For fuller particulars of this maker see Chapter 7.

MAIRE, NICOLAS, Mirecourt and Paris. Was a pupil of Jacques Lafleur but never did any work of great distinction.

MIQUEL, EMILE. A contemporary Mirecourt maker.

NÜRNBERGER, KARL ALBERT, Markneukirchen. Contemporary. A most finished workman and a clever imitator of the styles of various well-known makers. Has worked much for the trade. His best examples are frequently stamped with his name, and amongst these will be found bows which are fit to rank with some of the finest productions of the French school. There are other makers of the same family engaged in bow making.

PAJEOT. Worked in Mirecourt in the early part of the present century. An excellent maker. He taught Joseph Fonclause who is known to have made some of the finest bows bearing Vuillaume's stamp.

PANORMO. The quaint faceted bows of which I have given an example in Plate VIII. were made, as far as I have been able to ascertain, by George Louis Panormo, in the early part of this century. Details concerning this family are neither plentiful nor clear, but it is fairly certain that this bow maker was a son of Vincent Panormo of Palermo, Paris, Ireland, etc., who first made the name famous in the fiddle world. A description of the characteristics of his work will be found in Chapter VII.

Fleming mentions a George Louis Panormo as a *modern* maker in London, but I do not know of such a maker. I am informed on excellent authority that all the Panormo bows were made in Paris.

PECCATTE, DOMINIQUE. Born in 1810 and died in 1874 at Mirecourt. Details of his life and work are given in Chapter VII.

PECCATTE, FRANÇOIS ("PECCATTE JEUNE"), Paris. Born Mirecourt, 1820, died Paris, 1855. A good workman, whose best bows, though not well known in this country, are of nearly equal merit with his brother Dominique's. He worked for ten years with Vuillaume. Some of his bows are stamped with his name, the lettering of the stamp differing slightly from that employed by his more famous brother.

PECCATTE, CHARLES, Paris. Son of François. Born Mirecourt, 1850. A good workman, but not equal to the other makers of the name.

PELLEGRI, Italian, modern; neat workmanship.

PERSOIT. Worked in Paris about 1828 to 1841. He was employed largely by Vuillaume and most of his bows bear the latter's name, but he occasionally worked on his own account and then his work was stamped P.R.S.

PRICE, London. Contemporary, excellent maker. Pupil of Tubbs.

PFRETSCHNER, Markneukirchen. Contemporary makers, whose best work is of high merit and finish, though not quite equal to that of A. Nürnberger.

POISON, Paris. A really magnificent workman. He was employed largely by the firm of Gand and Bernardel, and the majority of his bows bear their stamp. One occasionally meets with a bow by this maker bearing his own name.

PUPINAT, Swiss. Middle of the present century.

RAKOWSCH, Paris. Modern.

RAU, AUGUST, Markneukirchen. Born 1866. A first-class workman. Worked much for Weichold of Dresden.

RONCHINI, Italian. Modern.

SCHWARTZ, GEORG FRIEDRICH, Strasburg. Born 1785, died 1849. Made some excellent bows marked "Swartz, Strasburg."

SIMON, P. Born at Mirecourt in 1808. Worked for D. Peccatte in Paris in 1838. After this he worked for Vuillaume for seven years. He then set up on his own account for some two years, and when D. Peccatte left Paris he took over the business in partnership with Henry. Three years later and he was again alone. His workmanship is always good and betrays Peccatte's influence.

SIRJEAN. French. Early part of the present century.

SÜSS, JOHANN CHRISTIAN, Markneukirchen. Born 1829. Died 1900. One of the best makers Germany has produced. Imitated the style of Tourte.

TADOLINI, IGNAZIO. Born at Bologna in 1791, died at Modena in 1873. Was established with his brother at the last-named town. Made some very fine bows but was not equal.

TOURNATORIS. French. Latter part of last century.

TOURTE. Eighteenth century, Paris. One of the best bow makers of the older type, chiefly known as the father of François Tourte.

TOURTE, SAVÉRE. Eldest son of the preceding and called "Tourte l'aîné," Paris.

TOURTE, FRANÇOIS, Paris. Brother of the above, the greatest of all bow makers. Born 1747, died 1838. For fuller particulars of his life and work see Chapter 6(Plates V. and VI.).

TUBBS, W., London. Early nineteenth century. Worked for Forster, Betts, Norris and Barnes. He was taught bow making by Edward Dodd.

TUBBS, JAMES. Son of the preceding. Born 1835. Died April, 1921. Many of his bows are graduated according to a system based on the calculations of W. S. B. Woolhouse, the mathematician (see Chapter VII). The Tubbs bows have qualities distinctly their own and when a player becomes thoroughly used to a "Tubbs" he rarely feels comfortable with even the finest bows of another make. Conversely, a player in the habit of using constantly any other bow experiences a slight feeling of strangeness on first trying a "Tubbs." The workmanship in a Tubbs bow is almost unique in its perfection. And there is a characteristic English solidity about the secure way in which all the fittings are adjusted. I have been an eye witness of the care and attention paid by his son, Mr. A. Tubbs to the work of repairing a bow that to the casual observer would seem past all treatment. His brother, C. E. Tubbs, was a good bow maker, but somewhat erratic.

VIGNERON, A. A modern French maker who turns out some extremely high class work.

VOIRIN, NICHOLAS FRANÇOIS. Another of the great Parisian bow makers. Learnt the craft in his native town, Mirecourt, where he was born in 1833. At the age of twenty-two he was employed by Vuillaume, with whom he worked for some fifteen years. It is believed that the finest bows bearing Vuillaume's name were made by Voirin. Some of his bows that were exhibited by Vuillaume in the Paris Exhibition in 1867 received honourable mention. I should say his work is more equal than that of any other maker. Of course, as with other popular makers, there are to be found plenty of worthless bows bearing the forged stamp, "N. F. Voirin, à Paris." His death, which took place in Paris in 1885, was very pathetic. He was walking along the Faubourg Montmartre on his way to the abode of a customer to whom he was taking a bow newly finished, when he suddenly fell down in an apoplectic fit. Fortunately his name and address, "Bouloi 3," was on the parcel containing the bow, and he was thus able to be taken home without delay. But how sad a home-coming! brought home in a dying condition to his wife whom he had left but a few minutes before in apparently good health. He died the same night.

VUILLAUME, J. B., Paris. This strange mixture of cunning and ability will be ever remembered as the craftiest of craftsmen. An undoubted genius as a violin maker, yet with all the tricks and subterfuges of the veriest charlatan. Concerning the real value of the historical details furnished to Fétis by Vuillaume I have spoken in Chapter V. Though it is possible that he had considerable practical knowledge of bow making, I do not think he actually made any bows. He exercised great judgment, however, in the employment of skilled workmen, whom he kept as a rule for a number of years—a fact that is sufficient to stamp him as a good and considerate employer. The most noted makers who worked for him were Fonclause, Peccatte, Persoit, Simon and Voirin. It will thus be seen that the majority of the bows bearing Vuillaume's name are of the best possible workmanship and quality. Unfortunately there are in this case also a number of forgeries on the market. The most noteworthy features in connexion with Vuillaume, as regards bows, are his curious inventions—the steel bow, the fixed nut, the curved ferrule, and the self-hairing bow. Of the steel bow, Mr. Heron-Allen says he has "never met with a specimen of so ponderous an eccentricity" except the one in South Kensington Museum. I have come across a number, and as they are tubular they are not at all as ponderous as the name of the material suggests. In fact I remember one that was very pleasant to play with. They are nearly always lacking in balance. The fixed nut was the result of an idea that the player should always have the same length of hair at his service. The curved ferrule was also a mistake, the idea being that it would be good to get a broad surface of hair on the string at the heel. The self-hairing bow was ingenious but of no practical value. These patents are detailed more fully in Part II. Vuillaume was born at Mirecourt on October 7th, 1798, and was the son of the carrier between that town and Nancy. He died at Paris in 1875.

WEICHOLD, Dresden. An excellent firm, who put their name on a superior class of "trade bow."

WILSON, JOHN JAMES THOMPSON, London. Born March, 1864, worked in his youth with James Tubbs, and later with C. E. Tubbs. Has worked much for the trade.

With this list of bow makers ends the historical section of these papers. As I have already explained, a perfect history of the bow is quite impossible to obtain, and all I have attempted has been to lay before my readers the facts I have accumulated. I have carefully abstained from promulgating any theories of my own with regard to the evolution of the bow (save in such cases where certain conclusions have been forced upon me by the evidence found) as from the conflicting nature of the records, I consider no one theory to be sufficient. There seem to have been a number of separate influences at work, the ultimate convergence thereof resulting in the production of the perfect bow as we now know it. If I have been unable to make a clear exposition of the bow's progress, I trust I have succeeded in showing the unprincipled elimination of contradictory details resorted to by earlier writers in order to achieve this desired end. And I hope it will be understood that this has not been done in the spirit of the small boy who, disappointed in his attempt to build a sand castle, derives an alleviative gratification from the destruction of the more imposing erections of his playmates.

PART II.
BOW MAKING.

CHAPTER IX.

MATERIALS—BRAZIL WOOD—HORSEHAIR—THE ACTION OF ROSIN.

It is curious to pass in review the strange events—the causes, heterogeneous and improbable, that have produced many of the most important results in the history of man. What fiddler, for instance, when indulging in the customary smoke after an evening's "grind," realises his indebtedness for half his enjoyment to an unscrupulous Genoese pirate of the fifteenth century? Yet, seeing that in addition to wooden nutmegs, banjoes and other blessings of civilization emanating from the New World, America gives us both tobacco and Brazil wood (the only material of which it is possible to make a thoroughly good bow), I think that, if I may liken the violinist's mind to a temple of many shrines erected to all those who have contributed to his welfare and enjoyment, there should be one niche reserved for Christopher Columbus of egg-balancing fame.

It is also of interest to note how, as soon as violinists were ready for a perfect bow, François Tourte appeared on the scene and provided the much desired article. How he experimentalized on common sugar-barrel wood I have already set down in its proper place. This was, of course, to gain proficiency in the use of his new tools. In his search after a wood that should contain the essential qualities of strength, lightness and spring, he made bows of many kinds of wood, but was not satisfied until he tried the red wood imported for dyeing purposes from Pernambuco. I am afraid there are few who reflect on the significance of the fact that the exact wood required *did* actually exist. Formerly the bow-maker had to buy the wood in the rough state just as shipped over, and then would begin the weary work of selecting those pieces suitable for his purpose. As a matter of fact they are few and far between, for this wood is particularly full of twists, knots and splits. Now this is done for him by firms who buy the raw material, select that with the desired straight grain and cut it into square rods ready for the craftsmen to work up into bows. A few years ago bow makers demanded very dense wood under the impression that it would be advantageous to have them as slender as possible, for the denser the wood the thinner must be the stick to preserve a normal weight. The fallacy of this method, however, soon made itself apparent, for, though you may thin down a stick *ad libitum*, the head *must* be a certain height and breadth, consequently these bows were all more or less top heavy. A much lighter variety of wood therefore is now being used, and I must say the appearance of some recent bows by our best English makers is extremely fine; there is a greater sense of proportion apparent to the eye as well as to the hand.

Some of the cheap German and French trade bows are made of what the dealers call Brazilette wood, a wood somewhat allied to the true Brazil wood, but totally lacking in spring or firmness. I wonder whether violinists often realise when they take up a bow how many remote parts of the earth have contributed to this little magic wand! Wood from the West, ivory from the East, mother-of-pearl from the sea, gold or silver from Eastern, Western, or, it may be, Antipodean mines; and, when we add thereto the hair from the horse's tail, we levy a tax upon the three kingdoms, vegetable, animal and mineral, to minister to our enjoyment.

As much discrimination has to be exercised in selecting the hair as in the case with the wood, for it is essential that every hair in the bow be absolutely cylindrical and of equal thickness throughout. These have to be sought for very carefully and are not so plentiful as one would suppose, for the shape of a hair is regulated by that of the pore from which it grows and these are seldom circular, many being flat on one side, some, even, square or triangular. It has been estimated that the proportion of suitable hairs is not more than ten per cent. Tourte, according to Fétis, always preferred French hair for his bows as he found it "larger and stronger than that of other countries." I believe at present a quantity of Russian hair is used.

Tourte's daughter was of great assistance to him in selecting and preparing the hair. His method was to thoroughly cleanse the hair with ordinary soap, then to soak it in bran water and then, after removing all foreign matter, to dip in "blue water." A few years ago some misguided people tried bleaching the hair chemically. This, however, made it quite dry and brittle, and it has happily been abandoned.

The average number of hairs in a bow now-a-days is from 150 to 200. In Tourte's day a similar number were used.

A few words on the structure and action of bow hair and the real part played by rosin may not be amiss. As Mr. Heron-Allen truly observes "it is astonishing how few violinists know anything about the mechanical and scientific action of powdered rosin on tone production." And for the laity he says again that many think, when they see a bow being rosined, that it is being "greased to make it go faster."

If we examine a hair microscopically we discover a surface covered with minute scales. Ordinarily these scales lie close to the main shaft, but when rosin is rubbed along the hair small particles get fixed under the scales causing them to stand up somewhat like the teeth of a saw. These erected scales act on the string like so many infinitesimal *plectra* and thus produce in perfection the sustained sound attempted in a grosser manner by the tremolo of the mandoline. It is simply a rapid series of shocks. A moment's consideration will suffice to realize that continuous pressure on a string would act as a deterrent rather than a promoter of vibration. In fact an unrosined bow gives continuous pressure and therefore produces no sound.

The hair is usually inserted in a bow in the natural position of its growth, *i.e.*, the root end at the top, thus, as the scales point downwards, giving the greatest attack to the down bow. Some have tried placing half one way and half the other but I do not think a very perceptible difference results from this proceeding.

CHAPTER X.

QUALITIES ESSENTIAL IN A BOW MAKER—SHAPING THE STICK—SETTING THE *Cambre*—THE FACES—THE TRENCHES—THE NUT.

The manufacture of the bow is an industry calling for rare qualities of patience and concentration on the part of its followers. The skill required is of quite a distinct kind. Strength and delicacy of hand must both be exceptionally pronounced, and mathematical accuracy of eye is essential. Delicacy of touch to readily appreciate the varying degrees of elasticity found not only in different sticks but often in the same piece of wood. Strength to work with precision in such hard wood. And for this kind of work the strength required is not that of the carpenter who can use the weight and swing of his body; it is, rather, a self-contained strength in which opposing forces must co-operate in order to ensure the absolute accuracy so indispensable in a bow. Then the sight must be of unerring judgment, for nearly all the work depends on the eye. Bow making is distinctly nervous work for it keeps the mind constantly alert.

I am indebted for most of the details given in this chapter to the late Alfred Tubbs, son of James, and a good workman, who died comparatively young in 1909. He told me that he only made one bow at a time for the reason that each stick has its own individuality, some intrinsic feature that has to be borne in mind through all the details of fitting, mounting and adjusting. The mind is apt to lose its certainty of retention when exercised on as few, even, as three sticks simultaneously. Therefore each bow is completed before the next is commenced.

Taking the rough stick as shown in Fig. 34, the first operation is that of "rounding the throat," in other words the square rod is made round for a few inches just below the rough block left for the head to be cut from, this portion being called by some the "throat," and by others the "neck" of the bow. After this the corners of the remaining square portion are planed away, thereby making the stick octagonal in section. Should it be intended that the finished bow be octagonal, naturally the throat is not rounded but the planing away of the corners is carried out with extreme care right up to the head. The next operation is to lay the pattern (Fig. 35) on the projecting block and, with a fine pointed pencil, to mark out the outline of the head. This is the only part of the work on the stick itself wherein the eye is assisted by actual measurement or pattern. The shaping, or modelling of the head, as also, later, the gradation in thickness of the stick depending entirely upon optic precision. The absolute accuracy of hand and eye required for such work is only to be attained by long years of constant application.

FIG. 34.   FIG. 35.

After roughly shaping the head comes the delicate operation of "setting." This is also known as putting in the "spring" or *cambre*. The principle upon which the amount of curve is determined is that an imaginary straight line drawn from the face of the head to the face of the nut shall coincide with the stick at the point of its greatest deviation from the horizontal. There is no fixed distance from either end for this extreme point of deviation to occur. It is a matter that rests entirely on the judgment of the maker, who, if thoroughly experienced, regulates the curve by any variation in rigidity he may discover in the stick. Thus should his observations point to the fact that a certain portion of the stick is slightly weaker than the rest, there will he put the greatest amount of "spring." It must be understood, however, that a good maker never uses a stick that is palpably unequal. He will only take this trouble to correct infinitesimal weaknesses (discernible only to a hand of great experience) in wood of exceptionally good grain. It is astonishing how many violinists seem to think good bows are made by accident. Few know that there are some men who can *make* a fine bow.

The prime factor in the "setting" of a bow is heat, by the judicious application of which the straight rod is made to assume and retain the desired *cambre*. The heat used now-a-days is that produced by an ordinary gas flame. Dry heat is absolutely essential, as the slightest moisture draws all the pigmentary matter out of the cells in the wood and leaves the bow as colourless and mean in appearance as a stick of deal. As it is, with dry heat even, the amount of colour exuded by a good stick during this process is quite enough to stain the hands a deep purple.

The great point to be observed in "setting" a bow is to make sure that the fibres are all heated equally right through to the centre of the stick. If this does not receive sufficient attention the bow can not possibly retain its curve, for the inner fibres that have not been affected by the heat will always be trying to resume their original straight position, and are bound ultimately to overcome the resistance of the heated outer fibres, with the result that the bow either becomes straight or warped and twisted, most probably the latter. To understand that this must be so it is only necessary to remember that any elastic rod, a walking stick for example, can be held so as to form a curve but as soon as the pressure is released it immediately recovers its normal state. This is what happens with the unheated inner fibres in an inferior bow. The constant strife of opposing forces *must* result in victory for the active force of the inner fibres over the passive resistance of the heated outer fibres.

For the operation of "setting"

FIG. 36.

the bow is left about half as thick again as the finished stick is intended to be: this to allow for scorching or burning the outer surface. When the "setting" is satisfactorily accomplished the stick is planed up round, after which the bottom trench is cut. This is the slot in which the screw-eye of the nut travels. Then the hole for the screw itself is drilled out in a lathe fitted with a "Cushman chuck." The next thing is to put on the "black face." This is a thin slab of ebony glued on to the under surface of the head, which helps to strengthen the head and forms a solid bed for the ivory or metal plate which forms the outer facing of the head. The ivory faces are cut out of the solid tusk to the shape shown in Fig. 36. They are glued on with the very best glue procurable and tied down with strong twine. This is another matter of extreme difficulty and delicacy, as ivory is a very stubborn material to work in and it is easy to crack it in forcing it down to the curve of the face, that is if it is sufficiently thick adequately to fulfil its original purpose as a strengthener and protector of the head. One often sees in cheap bows faces of ivory so thin as to show the ebony face through in a bluish tint. Such a face is of as much value to the bow as a piece of paper, but it was easy to put on!

Metal faces are growing more and more into favour but, personally, I prefer a substantial ivory face, for though the metal may be stronger in itself I think an ivory face well glued on is more homogeneous. The successive layers of ebony and ivory on the already hard wood forms a more equal gradation of density.

After both the faces are adjusted a circular hole is drilled in the head and then chiselled out square to form the top trench or box to receive the hair. The nut is then fitted. Many people imagine that even the best makers buy the nuts wholesale and fit the sticks to them, but good makers always make the nut for each bow as it is wanted. They can by this means better regulate the balance of the bow.

FIG. 37.

Fig. 37 shows a gauge to determine the various dimensions of the nuts of violin, viola and 'cello bows. Before the bow is finally "cleaned up" it is haired* and screwed to see if it is all true, for there may be something faulty in the *cambre* which can be corrected at this stage. If all is satisfactory the bow is finished and polished, the whole process, from the rough stick in Fig. 34 to the finished bow ready for the artist to melt, delight and amuse his hearers, being one day's work.

* For details of bow hairing see Chapter XII.

CHAPTER XI.

POSSIBLE REPAIRS—SPLICING—RENEWING CUPS—RESTORING THE NUT—RE-FACING.

Bow repairing is a matter calling for almost more skill than the actual manufacture of new bows, and it is one about which very hazy ideas exist outside the trade itself. One can divide violinists roughly into two sections. On the one hand there are those who believe anything is possible in this way, and on the other there are many who have no faith whatever in such repairs.

FIG. 38.

I recollect when only a lad meeting an elderly amateur violinist of the pompous class who not only was kind enough to pay the most embarrassing attention to my solos but further favoured me with his conversation and advice. "Now," said he, "you must get a steel bow; tell your father about it; absolutely necessary. You see this stick of a thing you are playing with" (alas, my cherished Lupot!) "is all very well *now*, but by-and-bye the hairs will come out and it will be worthless." I ventured to suggest that it could be re-haired. "Ah yes, yes, yes!" he replied, "I know it *can* be done, and it *is* done, very often, but it is never the same thing. No, once the hairs begin to go, there is nothing to do but buy a new bow, but if you have a steel bow the hairs cannot come out and you have an article that will endure in its original state all your life." (!)

I may observe that this gentleman had not the slightest commercial interest in steel bows.

I also came in contact once with an example of the opposite class. This gentleman had a little son who was in the habit of borrowing his father's violin bow surreptitiously for the purpose of perfecting himself in the useful art of single stick practice. The inevitable happened, and when I saw the bow it was proudly exhibited to me as an example of what could be done with a little ingenuity. The two halves of the broken bow had been well glued together, two steel pen nibs had been placed so as to form a sort of metal tube to protect the fracture, and the whole was bound securely with strong silk. In its owner's estimation it was "as good as ever, sir, as good as ever."

I propose to state here briefly what can be done and what is advisable to have done in the way of bow-repairing.

If a bow is broken in the upper part of the stick it is just possible to splice on a new head and throat, but it is not worth doing, for the *cambre* and balance of the original can never be reproduced. In the first place there is a different piece of wood which, however well matched, is bound to be sufficiently strange to disturb such a delicate instrument. And then the *cambre* of the new piece has to be set before it is joined on to the old stick and thus it becomes impossible to make a satisfactory curve throughout.

To re-adjust the original head is not feasible, as the only joint that will stand the strain to which a bow is subjected is a long diagonal one extending for several inches.

Splicing a new "handle" (Fig. 38*d*) is, however, frequently done, and is often advisable. It occasionally happens that a valuable bow becomes so worn by the pressure of the fingers or thumb, or by the friction of the nut and screw, as to be beyond the reach of the more usual repairs. It then becomes necessary to substitute a new handle, and this can be done by skilful repairers as to make absolutely no difference to the balance of the stick. The joint is in this case also a diagonal one extending usually from near the upper extremity of the "lapping" downwards for some four or five inches. It should be seen that the surfaces brought in contact in such a joint are so placed as to be perpendicular to the plane of the hair. Otherwise it cannot endure for any length of time.

FIG. 39.

Very often the original handle can be restored and made sound. Thus, when the screw hole becomes worn and the "cup" (see Fig. 39, which shows the two "cups," that at the extremity of the stick and that in the "tip") broken, it is customary to drill out the hole, turn up a piece of well-seasoned bow wood in the lathe to the exact diameter of the enlarged hole, and glue it well in place. When thoroughly dry a new screw hole of the original dimensions can be drilled just as in making a new bow. Sometimes, when there are cracks in the handle, the trench has to be filled up and re-cut, as is also done to the head if it is cracked through the pressure of the plug (Fig. 40*a*). Repairs to the nut are also done when the nut is original, *i.e.*, when it belongs to the bow and is of a distinguished maker. Old nuts frequently get cracked down the sides where they come in contact with the stick. In this case the worn part of the nut is cut away and new wood glued on and worked up to the original shape. I have seen a nut so restored by Mr. Tubbs in which it was absolutely impossible to discover where the new piece was joined on.

FIG. 40.

FIG. 41.

With regard to the screw hole, it often becomes worn to an oval shape just above the trench owing to the screw being too short. This is frequently found in old French bows, even by the best makers, and causes the unsightly tilting of the tip. In Fig. 41 is shown a section of the nut and handle showing the action of the screw and the way the hair is inserted. The screw in this diagram is the exact length necessary to prevent the wearing away of the hole described above.

Bow repairers are often perplexed as to their customers' meaning when sending instructions by post for the restoration of the "tip," as many people use this word to denote the extremity of the head (Fig. 40*d*).

This, however, is known to experts as the "peak," and the word "tip" is applied solely to the octagonal piece at the opposite end of the bow, by means of which the screw is turned and the tension of the hair regulated.

In some bows the octagonal portion, known as the handle (Fig. 38*d*) on which the nut travels has the lower face rather larger than the rest as in the section shown in Fig. 42. The object of this enlargement is to give the nut a broader surface to travel on and thus prevent the tendency to rock exhibited by some nuts. But, though there is some merit in the idea it has been found that the rocking can be avoided in a normal bow having the eight sides of the handle equal by extra care in fitting. And though the other pattern may be easier to fit in the first instance, the projecting sides of the nut that travel on the adjacent faces of the handle are very small and weak; consequently before long the nut shows longitudinal cracks at this part and becomes extremely rocky, though from a different cause.

One of the most frequent repairs is the operation of re-facing. The handsome central gasalier of the modern room is a great enemy to the violin and seems to lie in wait for the peak of an unwary violinist's bow. Fortunately the damage is not very serious, and an experienced bow repairer will not be long in restoring the head to its original elegance of outline.

FIG. 42.

CHAPTER XII.

RE-LAPPING—RE-HAIRING—CHOICE OF ROSIN.

The lapping frequently wears out and becomes a source of great irritation until one has an opportunity of having it newly done. For this reason a lapping of leather is the most convenient and economical, but nothing looks better than a good quality of silver cord, and when it is bound with leather just where otherwise it would suffer from the pressure and friction of the thumb nail it is really very durable. Messrs. W. E. Hill and Sons have an extremely handsome speciality in the way of lapping. This consists of whalebone, sometimes bleached or dyed, and is practically indestructible. Bound on in alternate strands of different colours it has a very effective and neat appearance.

Sometimes the ordinary thread lapping gets cut through and interferes with the player, and it is as well to know how to fasten it off at once. I will assume that it is cut at the end nearest the nut (where it usually happens). Take out the screw and wind the hair loosely but securely round the upper part of the bow. Then unwind the lapping for about an inch and a half. Take a piece of strong thread and double it, then place it on the bow with the doubled end towards the handle. Get a kind friend to hold the end of the lapping cord firmly and commence winding it on again evenly and *over* the doubled thread by slowly rotating the bow. When within half an inch of the end of the thread, take it all in your own hand and pass the end through the loop of doubled thread and, taking the loose ends of the thread that will hang out at the point where you started re-winding, pull the doubled thread smartly out. This brings the end of the lapping right through under the re-wound portion, where it will be held secure until again cut through by the thumb-nail. This is the method employed in fastening off new lappings. If you have not the time or patience to do it this way a little sealing wax will hold the loose end down during an evening's practice.

Considering that re-hairing is one of the most natural and most frequent events in the life of a bow, it seems somewhat anomalous to include it under the heading of "repairs." However, I will crave the reader's kind indulgence for so doing.

At the outset I must emphatically assert that I do not advise amateurs or artists to attempt to hair their own bows if any value attaches to them, for it is astonishing how soon even a fine bow will lose its *cambre* if persistently haired in an unskilful manner. It requires enormous experience to enable one to get the pull of the hair equal in every case, and the slightest extra pull on one side or the other gives the bow a twist that renders its action erratic and extremely disturbing to a good violinist. The preceding operation to re-hairing is that of unhairing. This is comparatively a simple matter. The hair is first cut off short at each end, then hair at the head is lifted up to disclose the plug (Fig. 40*a*). This is readily lifted out with a pointed tool, and the curled up knot lying beneath is pulled out. So much for the head. The nut is slightly more complex. First the ferrule (Fig. 41*d*) is pulled off and the slide (Fig. 41*f*) is pushed out. After this the hair is raised as with the head, and the plug (Fig. 41*e*) picked out in the same manner. The wedge in the nut (Fig. 41*c*) is used to spread the hair and keep it firm at the heel, to give a good attack for heavy down strokes. This is usually destroyed in unhairing, as it frequently has to be cut away, owing to its being glued into position.

The process of re-hairing is now identical with that of hairing a new bow in the first instance. Some keep the hair ready made up into "hanks" of the right quantity for a bow, and others have it in large bundles, pulling it out as required. One soon gets practice in this to judge by the eye alone how much will be sufficient. At one end it is tied securely with waxed silk or thread, and the short ends are cut off to within about a sixteenth of an inch from the thread. To prevent the thread being pulled off the end of the hair, the ends are burnt with rosin so as to spread them out slightly (very slightly) mushroom wise, over the thread binding. The usual way of doing this is to fill the short end—which resembles a small stencil brush—with finely powdered rosin and then, by pressing it against a red-hot iron, to shape it into a firm, unyielding knot. This knot is laid in the trench of the head, and the plug pressed firmly into position, so that its upper surface is exactly level with that of the plate or face. The hair, of course, must be brought over the wedge in an even ribbon. The hair should now be well combed with a fine comb and then steeped, coil fashion, in warm water for several minutes. It then should be thoroughly combed again from top to bottom, holding it firmly the while at the lower end. The nut is now placed in position with the screw-eye rather above the centre of the slot in which it travels, then a careful estimate is made of the length of hair required to go just far enough round the plug (Fig. 41*e*) to be secure, and a knot exactly like the one described for the head is made at the point decided on. This requires considerable experience, as it is very easy to make it too long or *vice versa*, both of which faults hamper the nicety of adjustment of tension required for some particular style of bowing technique. When this lower knot is made the ferrule is slipped over the hair, the knot is laid in the trench and the plug put in as before—the nut being completely detached from the stick. The nut is then re-adjusted and slightly screwed up. The hair is then combed again, the slide pushed in, and the ferrule slipped over the extremity of the nut. After this a thin wedge is driven in (behind the hair) usually with a spot of glue on the side next the hair, as at *c*, in Fig. 41. The bow is now haired, and all that remains to make it ready for use is to rosin it. As new hair never bites on a block of rosin, it is necessary to spread a quantity of powdered rosin on a card or sheet of stout paper and rub the hair over it till it is quite full; after this it will take freely from the block. A newly haired bow is always extremely rough and is apt to produce a harsh, scratchy tone, but this defect wears off in a very short time.

I must again repeat my opinion regarding the inadvisability of violinists hairing their own bows, and I have only given the above details to gratify the curiosity of those who like to know "how it's done."

It is extraordinary the number and variety of rosins in the market; some in most wonderfully contrived boxes designed to keep the rosin dust from making the fingers sticky, or—more probably—to *sell!* Of all the different patents in this way, I find the ordinary book-shape by far the most satisfactory. The first quality of rosin is prepared by boiling down Venice turpentine. In a certain authority on violin matters I read that many soloists of celebrity use common kitchen rosin, but I cannot say I have much faith in the source from whence he can have received such information. It is advisable never to change the rosin used until the bow is re-haired, as in each there is some slight difference in composition that may not harmonize with what is already on the bow.

CHAPTER XIII.

THE PERFECTION OF THE MODERN BOW—DR. NICHOLSON'S PATENT BOW—VUILLAUME'S INVENTIONS—SELF-HAIRING BOWS—A FOLDING BOW—THE "KETTERIDGE BOW."

It is worthy of note, as a testimony to the simplicity and perfection of the bow, that there have been so few attempts, since Tourte's day, to alter or "improve" it in any particular. The few experiments that have been made in this direction have in nearly every case proved failures and have sunk into speedy oblivion.

FIG. 43.

One of the most remarkable productions in this way was the ponderous monstrosity invented by one Dr. Nicholson (Fig. 43). This hideous and unwieldy weapon was put forth by its inventor as the only correct form for a violin bow! It had to be haired with precisely 150 horse hairs dyed red. The reasons for this and the eccentric curve of the stick are subtleties into which I dare not venture!

Vuillaume's erratic genius was responsible for sundry attempts at improving the bow, the most complex being the fixed nut. He was struck by the fact that with the ordinary nut advancing and retreating by the action of the screw it was possible for it to be not always mathematically in the same place. Also that as the hair gradually stretched by use, the length thereof increased as the same tension was obtained each time it was screwed up for use. This, of course, made a minute difference in the balance of the bow. He apparently considered this a serious defect and set about inventing a nut that should render the balance and the length of the hair immutable. This was his patent "*hausse fixé*." As the name implies the nut was a fixture externally but contained a smaller metal nut that travelled inside it. These nuts were very unsightly as they were much more bulky than the ordinary nut. It is curious that it never occurred to him that the movement of the internal nut would similarly affect the balance. A sort of windlass in the nut would have been more exact, but, as a matter of fact the difference is more theoretical than practical, and is imperceptible to the player, so the fixed nut, like many other examples of wasted ingenuity, died a natural death.

Another of Vuillaume's patents was the steel bow. This was often a handsome looking instrument. Some were "got up" to look like Brazil wood and others were of a bright blue. As this was the natural colour of the metal it was more commendable but had a very odd appearance. These bows were not much heavier, if at all, than the average bow as they were hollow throughout. They were deficient in balance and had one great drawback. Though stronger and tougher in one sense than the wooden bow they would not stand so much knocking about. A bow, even in the hands of those accustomed to handling them, is liable to have an occasional fall, and if not broken, is as good as ever; in fact a bow rarely breaks unless it falls peak downwards. On the other hand the steel bow would generally "kink" or get dinted and bent if it came in contact with anything in a fall and would then be entirely useless. A third mistake of Vuillaume's was the curved ferrule. Thinking it would be advantageous to give the player a good spread of hair at the heel he made a ferrule that gave the ribbon of hair as it left the nut something the appearance of the hair in the primitive Egyptian bow illustrated in Fig. 11. This is still to be met with in some cheap foreign bows. A further notion of his was calculated to be of great benefit to such players as might find themselves in out-of-the-way places with a bow in need of new hair and no *luthier* or bow-repairer within reach. This was the "patent self-hairing bow." Its principles were sometimes used in conjunction with the "fixed nut" and steel bows. The hair for this bow was sold ready made into ribbons of the exact length by having a small brass rod placed transversely at either end; these rods slipped into appropriately shaped notches in the head and nut and the bow was haired. It does not appear to have been satisfactory and has gone the way of the other innovations of this and other makers. One other thing in connexion with Vuillaume's bows I will mention here though it is not in the nature of an "improvement" properly so-called, albeit I have no doubt Vuillaume thought it a great embellishment. In the nuts of some of his bows, just where the mother-o'-pearl "eye" is usually placed, he had inserted a minute and powerful lens with a microscopic transparent portrait of himself that could be seen therein on holding the nut to the light. It was just like the views one sometimes sees in penholders brought as presents from popular seaside resorts.

I have recently heard of another variety of self-hairing bow patented in America, but have not yet seen one. From that country, where, so I have heard, the bows drawn are of quite exceptional length, emanated a patent bow wherein fine cords are substituted for hair and also a contrivance, whereby, when the hair becomes smooth and useless on the one side, it can be taken out, turned round and then enters on a rejuvenated existence the other way about.

To return to Vuillaume's patent bows. All of these, excepting the steel bows, are splendid sticks, for they were made by Simon, Fonclouse, and other noted workmen. It is therefore a profitable thing to have them altered into normal bows. This can be done by skilful workmen so that the bow is as good as any other ordinary bow by the same maker, and is free from the encumbrance of the patent.

G. Chanot, of Manchester, I am told, has a patent bow that is made to fold in two for convenience in packing for travelling purposes. The idea is not as original as its inventor may think, for the Japanese kokiu which is fast becoming obsolete had an extremely long and flexible bow that was jointed together like a fishing rod.

The "improved bow," patented by Chas. Ketteridge, is distinctly novel and has much to commend it. The hair in this bow is placed at such an angle that, though the player holds his hand in the usual position, the full width of the hair lies evenly on the string from end to end. It has been well spoken of by the press and several noted artists. For chord playing it possesses distinct advantages, and I should think it would be very useful for certain orchestral players; it does not, however, seem to have attracted more than passing attention.

Truly the "fiddlestick" is a magic wand in more senses than one. As mentioned above it is significant that so little has been attempted in the way of alteration or improvement, and it is still more so that of that little such a small proportion is worthy of a second thought. As Bach stands in relation to the fugue, as Beethoven to the symphony and Stradivari to the violin, so is Tourte to the bow. Superior alike to his predecessors and successors, he stands high poised upon the pedestal of his incomparable genius.

PART III.
THE ART OF BOWING.

CHAPTER XIV.

THE UNDECIDED ASPECT OF TECHNIQUE—IMPORTANCE OF A KNOWLEDGE OF THE ANATOMY OF THE HAND—THE FUNCTION OF THE THUMB—INDIVIDUALITY IN TECHNIQUE.

In treating of the somewhat complex and, in many details, highly-disputed subject of the functions of the bow, I shall prefer to handle the question in the abstract rather than to launch myself on the choppy sea of "technique"; a sea abounding in shoals, reefs, undercurrents and whirlpools; extremely difficult to navigate inasmuch as that no two charts agree. Consequently when the mariner launches his boat the danger to himself and his passengers is considerable. In plain English the difficulty of explaining all the well-nigh imperceptible differences of movement in bone and muscle required for the various styles of bowing is so enormous that he who attempts to do so on paper lies under the grave danger of being misunderstood, and the student under the scarcely less grave one of misunderstanding. The danger is reciprocative, just as, to return to my nautical simile, the peril of the helmsman is shared by each passenger if he by mischance steers upon a submerged rock.

Therefore, dear reader, I will survey the whole prospect from a secure coign of vantage upon the mainland, and trust my impressions thereof may prove of some slight service to you. As I have disclaimed all intention of making this portion of my work a handbook of bowing technique it seems superfluous to add that my observations are addressed more to the teacher than the student. I use these words in their accepted and arbitrary meanings for the sake of distinguishing between two separate classes. Of course, from the higher standpoint, a good teacher is always a student. If it were not so the following pages would be written to no purpose.

Some years ago a certain eminent M.D. collaborated with a more or less well known singing master in a work on the Larynx. The musical world talked of little else but vocal chords and soft palates for many months, and the musical press was teeming with correspondence in which the pros and cons of such studies were hotly discussed, many of the antagonistic writers opining that the knowledge of the anatomy of the throat would be of as much service to a vocalist as that of the hand to a violinist. Which reasoning sounds at first glance quite complete, yet, on examination, it will be observed that there is no such close analogy as these writers appeared to think. To begin with, in singing the mind only occupies itself with the sound produced. To learn singing is to practise mimicry. We cannot determine the position of the vocal chords before producing the note. Our consciousness begins at the other end; the mind conjures up a certain ideal sound which we attempt to realize vocally; if the desired *timbre* is produced the laryngeal action is correct. With the violin thought commences with the means. The hand is trained; we say set the fingers so, and the thumb so. Now practice; when the action is perfect the tone will be right. Briefly in singing we strive for the tone and the action follows, in the violin we strive for the action and the tone follows. Thus it is clear that a knowledge of the structure of the hand is of distinct value to a violinist—in particular, a teacher—while, on the other hand, the knowledge of the anatomy of the throat can be little more than interesting to the vocalist.

A knowledge of the structure and functions of the various parts of the hand on the part of a teacher would smooth over many disheartening experiences of his pupils. Just as it is of value to study the mental characteristics of a pupil so, also, is it of value to thoroughly examine his physical peculiarities. I wonder how many violin teachers have noticed, or have profited by so noticing, that no two hands are alike, or that thumbs are of different lengths and set on in various degrees of opposition to the fingers. It is seldom that such apparently unimportant details are observed by teachers, the majority of whom make all their pupils hold the bow alike, long thumbs or short thumbs it makes no difference. I remember having for a pupil a young lady who had been taught to hold her bow at the extreme tips of her fingers. Naturally she gained no facility and every attempt at semiquavers sent the bow flying across the room to the imminent danger of the teacher's optics. I surmised the cause of this eccentricity and was ultimately able to verify my conjectures. The master who had been so conscientious in making her hold the bow in this strained and ungainly position was blessed with an abnormally long thumb; the pupil's thumb was short. What came natural to the one was a strain on the other.

The function of the thumb is that of a pivot; a fulcrum. The bow is a lever resting thereon, and its pressure on the string is regulated by the first and second fingers on the one side and by the third and fourth on the other. It would thus appear that the best place for the thumb would be exactly between the second and third fingers. But it is not given to every thumb to drop *naturally* into this position. And here is to be noted the germ of facility in bowing. Every thumb closes naturally on a certain spot; it may be on the second finger, or on the third. If the former it can be made to rest on the third or even the fourth without apparent effort, but minute observation will detect an infinitesimal strain when the thumb is taken beyond its natural resting place. Therefore I maintain that the best position for the thumb is to be determined by examination of the hand and thumb, and will differ slightly in each individual player. It is curious to note how many teachers, some of extreme eminence, take such pains to perpetuate their own bad habits in their pupils under the impression that they are teaching a perfect and superior technique. I am afraid that it sounds somewhat of a heresy to speak of great players and teachers having "bad habits"; the expression is, perhaps, rather strong, but what I refer to is the "personal equation." Such a player has a tendency to part his fingers, another elevates the fourth finger in certain passages, this one has a peculiar movement of the elbow, etc., etc. All these divergencies from rigid and pedantic technique being the result of their several physical differences. When these men prove themselves great artists and attain high positions as teachers their advice is sought on matters of technique. Finding themselves oracles they first consult the oracle by aid of looking glasses, analyse in this way their own actions, and then the one who parts his fingers lays it down as a law that the fingers should be parted, and the one with the peculiar movement of the elbow will not rest until all his pupils have acquired the same eccentricity. I will quote another example of this sort of thing that came under my own observation some years ago. It deals with the left hand, but displays the spirit so well that I feel it is not out of place in this connexion. A thin, delicate lad, with fingers "like needles"—as a brother violinist described them to me—was sent to a German professor whose digits resembled nothing so much as the handles of table knives. This was an excellent violinist, or rather "geiger," for the Germans make this distinction, but owing to the size of his fingertips he could only play semitones in the third position by removing the finger stopping the lower note while putting down the higher one. If he retained the second finger on E on the A string, third position, the third finger would fall too sharp for F natural. This seemed to him such an unalterable law of nature that he made the lad do the same, notwithstanding that the boy could have stopped quarter tones with ease had they been wanted!

Had this man made even a superficial study of the hand he would have been spared much profanity and the pupil much heartache and disappointment. Tuition is twofold. There is direct teaching and there is development. The seed is sown and then the soil is watered and tended in the manner calculated to nourish and develop the particular plant to the best advantage. Again, the gardener does not plant his roses in damp shady corners or his ferns in sand.

Teachers require to use more of the gardener's judgment. They must cease to look upon their pupils as defective copies of themselves and must not fit them out with technique as soldiers are with clothing. The technique should be made for the particular player. A violinist with an ill-fitting technique is about as elegant as a short man in clothes intended for a tall one, or vice versa. Many cases of bad or defective technique are directly attributable to the teacher's want of perception of "fit."

Thus we see players whose natural movements are bold and free trussed up in a small and finicking technique, and others whose bent is towards neatness, struggling manfully with a cumbersome "large style." I have heard a "gentleman" defined as "a man who wears clothes that belong to him." Similarly we may say that a good violinist is one whose technique belongs to him. Every movement should come naturally, it should be as much a part of his personality as his tone of voice or the glance of his eye, and it should be the teacher's aim to develop this personality and not to stifle it as is too often the case. Of course great judgment is required in this development, or the personality will become marked mannerism, than which nothing could be worse. True art always displays a certain reticence; excess at either end of the gamut of emotion is avoided. Calmness is not coldness, and passion carried too far becomes caricature. Tone must be developed also, but it should always be borne in mind that exertion is not power; a mistake too frequently made. How often do we see a well meaning but physically weak player trying to tear the tone out of a violin by "main strength." Such efforts are useless, particularly when practised on a fine violin. A really good instrument is of too sensitive an organisation to respond to bullying. Teachers cry out to their pupils sometimes "lay it on!" "pull it out!" and other contradictory sounding phrases with the same meaning, and occasionally such admonitions and encouragements bear good fruit, but there is always the danger of "effort" being engendered thereby. There should be no effort in art. Effort, too, defeats its own ends. It weakens; exercise strengthens. Therefore let the strength with which to "lay it on" or "pull it out" be gradually and naturally developed by constant and gentle practice. The muscles will gain strength thus, and the result will be a full round tone, capable of every inflection and free from everything like harshness.

Power should be implied rather than displayed. The instrument will then respond freely and fully as a woman to the caress of a strong manly arm.

CHAPTER XV.

BOWING HISTORICALLY CONSIDERED—
THE OLDEST ENGLISH VIOLIN METHOD—SYMPSON'S INSTRUCTIONS IN BOWING—THOSE OF MACE (1676)—THOSE OF VARIOUS MODERN MASTERS.

If the history of the bow's development *per se* presented a misty aspect we must not be surprised to find that of bowing similarly obscure.

Just as the violin arrived

FIG. 44.

at its state of greatest perfection long before the bow developed into a fitting companion.

When we consider the enormous progress in left hand technique accomplished by the earlier violinists and 'cellists, such as Corelli, Tartini, Bach, and a host of others, it seems incomprehensible that the bow should have so long remained in such a comparatively crude and primitive condition, and its mode of use so limited and undecided.

The best drawing I have seen of the manner of holding the bow in playing a higher pitched viol is in a miniature representation of a state banquet in the fifteenth century, from which I extract the player shown in Fig. 44.

The evidence of drawings, sculptures, etc., in the earliest days of rebecs and viols, if not reliable in the representation of the bow itself, are still less so when it comes to the question of handling the same. With the smaller viols, the thumb (such an important member) is naturally invisible, and the effect is usually that of a clenched fist. It seems to have been the general rule with all the viols of lower pitch that were held perpendicularly, to hold the bow underhand as described by Sympson in 1759 (Fig. 45). But the third drawing in Fig. 18 is remarkable alike for the modernness both of the bow and the posture of the hand holding it. This is on a par with the early bows with screw-nut and *cambre* described in the first section of this work. I cannot think it likely that the sculptor saw anyone playing a bass viol in this manner. Whether this representation was the result of gross ignorance or prophetic inspiration I leave to the reader to decide.

FIG. 45.

Of course the manner of holding the bow for the smaller viols would have approximated more nearly to that which obtains on the violin at the present day, as the underhand position would have been extremely inconvenient, and even impossible.

The earliest English method for the violin known is that contained in the second book of "An Introduction to the Skill of Musick, in Three Books," published in 1654 by John Playford.

Here the violin is just tolerated in a sort of appendix to the more important subject of the "Treble, Tenor, and Bass Viols." It consists chiefly of various methods of ensuring accuracy in tuning the fifths, and the question of bowing is summarily treated as follows:—

"The *Bow* is held in the right Hand, between the ends of the Thumb and the 3 Fingers, the Thumb being stay'd upon the Hair at the Nut, and the 3 Fingers resting upon the Wood. Your *Bow* being thus fix'd, you are first to draw an *even Stroak* over each *String* severally, making each *String* yield a clear and distinct sound."

Of the Treble Viols very little is said on the subject of bowing, the most complete instructions on that head being given for *the* viol *par excellence*, the viola da gamba. In treating of this glorious instrument the older writers spared no pains to make their directions as complete as possible. Thus Sympson in his "Division Viol"—first published in 1659—says:—

"Hold the Bow betwixt the ends of your Thumb and two foremost fingers, near to the Nut. The Thumb and first finger fastened on the Stalk; and the second finger's end turned *in* shorter, against the Hairs thereof; by which you may poize and keep up the point of the Bow. If the second finger have not strength enough, you may joyn the third finger in assistance to it; but in Playing Swift Division, two fingers and the Thumb is best.... When you see an even Number of Quavers or Semiquavers, as 2, 4, 6, 8, you must begin with your Bow forward; yea, though the Bow were imployed forward in the next Note before them. But if the number be odd, as 3, 5, 7 (which always happens by reason of some Prick-Note or odd Rest) the first of that odd number must be played with the Bow backward. This is the most proper motion of the Bow, though not absolutely without some exception; for sometimes the quickness of the Notes may force the contrary. Also quick Notes skipping from the Treble to the Bass, and so persued, are best express'd with contrary Bows."

All of which is very clear and logical. The way he balances up the relative claims of a stiff or loose elbow is, however, distinctly amusing, as witness the following:

"——you must stretch out your Arm streight, in which posture (playing long Notes) you will necessarily move your shoulder Joint; but if you stir that Joint in Quick Notes, it will cause the whole body to shake; which (by all means) must be avoyded; as also any other indecent Gesture. Quick Notes, therefore, must be expressed by moving some Joint near the Hand;* which is generally agreed upon to be the Wrist. The question then arising is about the menage of the Elbow Joint; concerning which there are two different opinions. Some will have it kept stiff; insomuch, that I have heard a judicious violist positively affirm, that if a Scholar can but attain to the playing of Quavers with his Wrist, keeping his Arm streight and stiff in the Elbow-Joint, he hath got the mastery of the Bow-Hand. Others contend that the motion of the Wrist must be strengthened and assisted by a compliance or yielding of the Elbow-Joint unto it; and they, to back their Argument, produce for instance a person famous for the excellency of his Bow-Hand using a free and loose Arm. To deliver my own opinion: I do much approve the streightness of the Arm, especially in Beginners, because it is a means to keep the Body upright, which is a commendable posture. I can also admit the stiffness of the Elbow, in smooth and Swift Division; for which it is most properly apt; but Cross and Skipping Divisions cannot (I think) be so well express'd without some consent or yielding of the Elbow-Joint unto the motion of the Wrist.... This motion or looseness of the Wrist I mention, is chiefly in *Demi-semiquavers;* for, in *Quavers,* and *Semiquavers* too, we must allow so much stiffness to the wrist as may command the Bow *on* and *off* the String, at every Note, if occasion so require."

* "*Some* joint" is very good; it gives such liberty in the way of choice.

This must have been rather a crude form of *spiccato*. It is, however, plainly evident that with heavy bows, destitute of elasticity, and held underhand, it was quite impossible to allow the bow to rebound naturally from the string for this effect.

Mace, whose book, "Musick's Monument," is one of the most amusing works extant, in speaking of the bowing of the viol, *i.e.*, viola da gamba, or, as he calls it, "the generous viol," quotes Sympson's direction for holding the bow and then adds:—

"Yet I must confess, that for *my own Part*, I could never *Use it so well* as when I held it 2 or 3 *Inches off the Nut* (more or less) according to the *Length or Weight of the Bow*, for *Good Poyzing of It:* But 'tis possible, that by *Use* I might have made It *as Familiar to* Myself, as It was to *Him.*"

He, also, was greatly exercised in his mind as to the stiffness or the reverse of the elbow, and delivered himself thuswise thereon:—

"So likewise, for the *Exact Straitness of the Bow-Arm*, which some do *Contend for*, I could *never do so well*, as with my *Arm* (*straight enough, yet*) *something Plying, or Yielding to an Agile Bending:* and which I do conceive most *Familiarly Natural.* (For I would have no *Posture, Urged, Disputed,* or *Contended for;* that should *Cross,* or *Force Nature.*")

There is much to commend in the spirit of this last sentence. The hand and arm should never be made to do anything that is unnatural. But herein must be exercised the greatest possible judgment that the unfamiliar be not mistaken for the unnatural.

Returning to the position of the thumb in violin playing we find nearly every teacher insisting on a different posture. In the "Méthode de Violon," by Baillot, Rode and Kreutzer, it is set down as being correct to have the thumb opposite the middle finger. David, in his "Violin School," says that the thumb should be opposite the *first* finger. This is to my mind most extraordinary, and I can hardly conceive it possible that so great a violinist and teacher could have maintained such an unscientific method to be correct. The loss of leverage resulting from the thumb being so far forward would be almost certain to cause the elbow to rise and give, by the dead weight of the arm, the pressure that should come from the sentient elasticity of the first and second fingers. De Beriot says the thumb should be between the second and third fingers, which is naturally the best position. Papini, with greater perception of the fact of anatomical difference in hands, says the thumb should be as near the centre of the four fingers as possible.

In all questions of technique it is possible to determine the exact best mode of procedure. But unless the hand be perfectly fitted thereto, the rule should be relaxed, for insisting on positions that are even slightly strained (though possibly, quite comfortable to a differently constructed hand) can only do harm.

CHAPTER XVI.

THE FINGERS OF THE RIGHT HAND—DIFFERENCES OF OPINION THEREON—SAUTILLÉ—THE LOOSE WRIST.

The functions of the right hand fingers are twofold. At times they act in conjunction with each other and at others, in opposition. Some writers say that the two outer fingers are the holding fingers, and others contend that the two inner fingers are alone concerned in this service. This difference of opinion is to me just as absurd as the arguments anent the wrist and elbow of the old violists. As a matter of fact both theories are right. The difference being that, in the question of holding, the action of the outer fingers is passive while that of the inner fingers is active. To go more into detail, in soft passages the bow simply rests supported by the three points of contact with the thumb, first and fourth fingers. The inner fingers then taking little or no part in the matter. This action of the outer fingers I say is passive as the bow is not actually *held* but simply rests on the thumb, the two outer fingers merely preventing it from falling to one side or the other. Occasionally these two fingers will act in concert or opposition, according to the requirements of expression and phrasing. When playing loudly it becomes necessary that a more decided purchase of the bow be maintained, especially in rapid *forte* passages. Then the inner fingers come into play and hold the bow firmly against the thumb. The two outer fingers then are solely concerned with regulating the pressure and preserving the elasticity of the stroke, which is lost in a firm grip only.

These slight differences of action in my opinion can not be *practised*. They are the outcome of years of grind. They come, and when they are firmly established we can analyse them. To gain the mastery of the bow one must begin at the bottom and be content to work gradually up to the topmost rung (or thereabouts!) of the ladder. I often meet with amateur violinists who try to begin at the top. The consequences of this proceeding are distinctly more certain, for when starting at the bottom it is not always assured that much upward progress will be made, whereas, by the opposite method the descent will be certain and considerable!

Nothing is more hopeless than the attempts some amateur violinists make to acquire certain styles of bowing simply by mentally mastering the various actions by which it is produced.

Sautillé, one of the easiest forms of bowing, suffers most from this sort of thing. It is no uncommon thing to see an amateur diligently practising the action of lifting the bow off the string and putting it on again after each note, thinking that if he keeps on long enough—say ten minutes a day for a fortnight—that he will acquire a perfect mastery of this much desired effect. To practice *Sautillé* in this manner is the way *not* to gain it. It is the outcome of the perfect action of the entire arm. When that is attained you will have the *Sautillé*. Then, and then only, will a little specialized practice help to perfect the movement. Some pupils I have had who possessed the *Sautillé* by nature and never understood the difficulty experienced by others who had to wait for it. The best way to acquire this as the result of a perfect bow arm is to practise the following:

Try it first on the D string. Use whole bows, freely and firmly, for the semibreves, slightly less for the minims, the middle third for the crotchets, and an inch or two for the quavers, reducing it still further as the pace increases. The pupil must abandon all thought of *making* the bow jump, also he must avoid pressing it on the string. The whole action must be free and bold and the tempo for this exercise should be not slower than M.M. crotchet = 100. At first it will be found impossible to get as far as the semiquavers without some confusion. At the first sign of irregularity the pupil should stop, pause a moment, and then recommence with the semibreves. It should be seen that the bow is not gripped too tightly through over-anxiety or excitement. It will need patience on the part of teacher and pupil alike, but both will be gratified when suddenly the bow is seen to jump naturally and the *Sautillé* is won.

There is one phrase in connexion with bowing that irritates me greatly, and that is a "loose wrist." As a technicality it is of course all right, but the insisting on the literal application of the term has been a stumbling block to many violinists. Ladies have come to me saying, "Do you think my wrist loose enough for me to play the violin?" Accompanying the query with a violent flapping of the hand that would almost make one think they were desirous of emulating the lobster's ability to cast away a claw at will. Upon making such persons hold a pencil or penholder (I dared not let them handle a bow!) it was found that the wrist became stiff and unyielding. The wrist that was loose when all the muscles were flaccid became rigid when a few were exerted sufficiently to hold a light object.

Thus it will be seen that the apparent looseness of a violinist's wrist is not really such, but is the dominating of one set of muscles by another. Many teachers say that one should have the thumb tight and the wrist loose. A manifest absurdity when one considers that a most important thumb muscle extends right across the wrist. It should therefore be well understood that what is implied by the technical expression "loose," is, in reality, "control." If it were really looseness, it would present no difficulty to any one not afflicted with an ossification. It is to gain this extreme independence of each set of muscles that long years are taken up in monotonous exercises. The arm of a violinist has to be trained in a manner directly opposite to that of an athlete. In the latter we find an exemplification of the saying, "Unity is Strength." All the muscles act in perfect accord to the same end. With the violinist, on the other hand, there is a constant opposition of forces; the larger muscles are kept down and many smaller muscles are developed that have lost all use in the arm of an athlete.

Concerning the fingers of the right hand I advocate holding them close together—not cramped, but just lightly touching. Some players recommend the parting of the first finger from the others as giving greater leverage over the bow. It certainly has that effect, but I advise it to be used very sparingly and in fortissimo passages only. It is a license one may admit in an artist, but to my pupils who are in the earlier stages I entirely forbid it. I should only permit it in the case of a thumb so short as not to reach far enough into the centre of the hand to give the right amount of control. If a pupil is taught from the first to use this extreme leverage he is likely to develop a rough tone. When he has attained the mastery of the bow he can use his own judgment as to the occasional employment of this reserve force. These remarks I apply also to violoncello bowing. Unless the pupil's hand be weak the first finger should be held back until the whole art of bowing is mastered. All these observations are addressed to soloists: in orchestral work such retention of force is unnecessary. I notice that where players use up all the available leverage of the hand from the outset, they are compelled to employ the weight of the arm to reinforce it for special effects. Another reason—and an important one—for keeping the fingers together, is that of appearance. Nothing is more unsightly than to see the fingers of the right hand spread out claw fashion, and I quite concur with Sympson that no posture or movement should offend the eye.

CHAPTER XVII.

THE IMPORTANCE OF THE SLOW BOW—THE RAPID WHOLE BOW—STACCATO—BOWING STUDIES AND SOLOS—CONCLUSION.

Returning for a moment to the anxiety of the average fiddler to acquire a good *Sautillé*, it seems to me absurd that such importance should be attached to it when, in reality, the test of a violinist's ability lies in his command of "slow bows." Too much attention cannot be paid to the study of sustained bowing which can be practised in a variety of ways. Firstly, long drawn semibreves—at one of the Continental Conservatoires they make the violin students play scales of two octaves, taking one bow to each note, the same to last *two minutes*, thus the whole scale, ascending and descending, occupies one hour! The command obtained by this sort of work is enormous. To vary the monotony of semibreves the student can then play scales in semiquavers, making one bow last out ten, twelve, or more scales in two octaves. Another useful variety of the same thing is to practise some succession of notes in which the bow requires to continually pass from one string to the next, such as:

These should be played as many times as possible in one bow. Here the command of the bow on the string is not only greatly increased, but the wrist is well exercised at the same time.

The same thing should be carried out on the third and fourth strings thus:

It is a good thing to make the pupil (if endowed with sufficient intelligence) work out a series of such mechanical exercises, he will this way take a much greater interest in the work, a point to which I attach great importance, for I consider physical exercises, however conscientiously carried out, do little good if the mind is fatigued or absent.

Of scarcely less importance is the study of rapid whole bows. The pupil should be made to draw the bow from end to end as rapidly as he can without *losing control of the bow*, and it must be seen that the pressure does not vary in any way. The bow should be set on firmly at the heel, held there for, say, a crotchet, then drawn, without any swelling of the tone in the centre of the bow, smartly to the point where it must stop suddenly without any change of pressure. This is not found an easy thing to accomplish, but "perseverance overcometh all difficulties." The teacher must not be satisfied until the pupil can draw a rapid up or down stroke stopping so suddenly and firmly as to make the note sound as though cut off. In practising this, the bow should remain firmly on the string between each stroke; whether the bow travels or is stationary the pressure must be unchanged.

Staccato bowing is a much misunderstood branch of technics; I do not mean the detached staccato, but that form in which a series of notes is played in one bow yet have a detached effect on the ear. It is a pity that one word should have to stand for two totally different forms of bowing. I have heard and read many varying descriptions of the "bowed-staccato" and its method of production. Of course it is highly probable that some players attain it differently to others, but as I see no anatomical reason for such differences of action it seems a waste of energy to mechanically produce what already exists in nature. I have no doubt a great deal of this gratuitous variegation of staccato technique comes from teachers not fully understanding their own movements, or perceiving a portion of the action required and laying all stress on that one feature alone. But unless one goes to the prime source of the matter a perfect staccato cannot be attained.

This most important factor, as I should have thought everyone of common sense would at once perceive, is nothing less than the wrist. Yet I have known some teachers who confine their attention to the action of the fingers, letting the wrist follow as best it can. It is from such teachers, usually, that we receive the preposterous statement that the upper half of the bow only should be used for this bowing; some, even, limiting it still further to the up-bow. Now if the wrist be first well exercised the co-operation of the fingers will come naturally, and a perfect staccato from end to end in either up or down stroke will be attained.

It should be practised slowly and firmly at first on one note thus:

The bow remaining on the string between each note. The action is really no different to ordinary bowing; it is simply a short crisp stroke of about an inch in length, a short interval of silence (without lifting the bow) and then another similar stroke in the same direction, this being continued to the end of the hair. The part played by the forefinger is to impart a certain "attack" to each note, and is best produced by a slight turn of the wrist instead of an independent pressure of the finger itself. This "attack" is what the Germans call "ansatz," and consists in making a slight sound at the initial impulse of each note somewhat resembling the hard pronunciation of the letter "K." This is a most important sound, and one that adds greatly to the crispness of one's playing. It should be produced in the hand, however, as if the arm is called on for this purpose the tone will become gritty and harsh. In commencing the study of staccato bowing it is well to confine oneself to the up-bow form at first. Great care must be exercised when reaching the lower half of the bow that the notes remain of equal duration and loudness. Just below the centre of the bow there is found a curious turning point, a sort of corner that is very difficult to get round. It is even more noticeable in down bow staccato.

This turning point is in the wrist, for at that part of the stroke the most important change in the position of this joint takes place. Therefore, as the muscles are so occupied in their internal movements, they are not so ready to control the tendency to vibrate in the bow. Thus, then, as a bad bow is nowhere so easily controlled as a good one, some inferior bows become quite unmanageable when the attention of the wrist muscles is so divided. Consequently it is useless to attempt the attainment of staccato without first being provided with a thoroughly well-balanced bow. In commencing the down bow staccato, all tendency to lean on the string and so drag the bow along in a series of jerks must be checked at once. The bow should be lightly carried at the heel. This will seem difficult, but practice will be well repaid.

It may not be out of place to give here a short list of studies and solos that are concerned chiefly with the art of bowing. Of course bowing studies are also to be found in all good schools and books of studies.

CASORTI, "The Technic of the Bow."
DANCLA, "L'Art de l'Archet" (quite easy).
HAAKMAN, "Steadiness and flexibility of the Bow."
MEERTZ, "Twelve Etudes Elementaires" (giving the six fundamental bowings).
PAPINI, "L'Archet" (the most complete work on the subject).
POZNANSKI, "The Violin and Bow" (contains excellent photographs of positions).

Sautillé can be studied in a pleasing manner by practising pieces of the "Moto Perpetuo" type. Of these the best are those by Paganini, Ries, Moszkowski, Papini, G. Saint-George and E. German.

Of solos devoted to particular forms of bowing, the most notable are:
DE BERIOT, "Le Tremolo."
KONTSKI, "La Cascade" (tremolo).
PANOFKA, "Le Staccato."
PRUME, "Les Arpèges."
VIEUXTEMPS, "Les Arpèges."
VIEUXTEMPS, 1st Concerto in E (staccato).
BAZZINI, "Ronde de Lutins" (saltando staccato).

In an earlier section of this work I alluded to the bow as being "tongue-like"; it is something more, for it is also the breath of the violin. As breathing is to a vocalist so is bowing to a violinist. It governs the phrasing, or, rather, is governed by it in the first instance and then controls its delivery to the listener. Thus it will be seen that too much attention cannot be paid to the real Art of Bowing. By which I do not mean the brilliant technical feats of *arpeggio, staccato, tremolo, etc.*, but the pure legato bowing of cantabile passages. It is in such song-like movements that the true artist reveals himself by the nearness with which he approaches that highest of all musical instruments, the human voice. Pure liquid tone, the inflexions suggested rather than insisted on, clear phrasing and an avoidance of all extravagance are the hall marks of an artist, and not the possession of brilliant technique alone. To those who are content with superficial glitter electro plate is as good as sterling metal. But critics of discernment (by which I do not mean *all* those who write concert notices for the daily papers) require something of more lasting value.

THE END.

www.ingramcontent.com/pod-product-compliance
Lightning Source LLC
Chambersburg PA
CBHW070608201224
19312CB00033B/805